THE CIVIL WAR DIARY
of
WILLIAM R. DYER

A Member of
FORREST'S ESCORT

WAYNE BRADSHAW

ISBN: 1-4392-3772-7
ISBN-13: 9781439237724
Library of Congress Control Number: 2009903809

Visit www.booksurge.com to order additional copies.

TABLE OF CONTENTS

DEDICATION

To My Confederate Ancestors:

**James Edward Bradshaw
Company C
15th Consolidated
Tennessee Cavalry**

and

**Sylvanus Sullivan
Company A
41st Tennessee Infantry**

FOREWORD

William R. Dyer was a member of Confederate General Nathan Bedford Forrest's Escort. The diary was originally that of Isaac B. Appleton, a Federal soldier from Highland Park, Lake County, Illinois, a member of the 22nd Wisconsin Volunteers. Appleton was evidently killed or wounded or simply lost the diary around Brentwood, Tennessee about January 31, 1863. Dyer came into possession of the diary and made all entries after that date. Dyer is listed as being present at Gainesville, Alabama at Forrest's surrender in 1865, but the diary ends abruptly with the entry dated August 11, 1864.

The unedited diary is presented first. Dyer makes brief entries almost daily from February 1863 until August 1864. He spells a number of words incorrectly but phonetically enough for us to understand. Dyer incorrectly identifies a few locations and landmarks, but this is understandable under the circumstances. He and his comrades were usually in unfamiliar territory, riding and fighting, underfed and short on sleep. Keeping up with Nathan Bedford Forrest was no picnic.

The edited version of the diary is an attempt to clarify and enhance Dyer's story and give the reader insight into Forrest's remarkable accomplishments. Spelling is corrected. Some punctuation and capitalization is added.

Dyer provides unique insight into the daily uncertainty, sorrow, and boredom of a Confederate cavalryman. The events he mentions (an opportunity to attend church, etc.) are a clear read on the development of his priorities as the war progressed. Given his place in the great drama, Dyer's diary is remarkable for the things not mentioned ! Why did Gould shoot Forrest ? Why were his officers under arrest for two weeks ? He leaves us wanting more.

Enjoy the ride.

ACKNOWLEDGEMENTS

In 1983 Bob Womack of Murfreesboro, Tennessee was kind enough to give me a copy of William R. Dyer's Civil War Diary. He had borrowed the original from two ladies in Eagleville, Tennessee and typed it out. I read it with interest and some amusement and put it away with my collection of civil war material. In 2008 while reading a journal from the civil war era I remembered my copy of Dyer's Diary. After reading it again, I decided to edit and perhaps publish it.

I've gotten good advice from Capt. Brent Lokey, USAF, Ret. of Shelbyville, Tennessee. Brent is an expert on Nathan Bedford Forrest and freely shares his knowledge with others.

The talented Lisa Turner of Tracy City, Tennessee was kind enough to do the sketch for the book's cover.

I thank my wife, Nancy for her patience with my dual obsessions – the Civil War and baseball.

I hope you find this work interesting and that it will spark more interest in the civil war's western theatre of operations.

Wayne Bradshaw
Monteagle, Tennessee
November 2008

THE CIVIL WAR DIARY OF WILLIAM R. DYER

Unedited

January 1863

01.01.1863   Danville Ky. New Year in the army – Business very brisk – wrote orders all day – got a letter from Birn at   Mr. Blake got here from home

01.02.1863   Pleasant day – prepared orders for pay day all day no letters for me to night   Traded pistols with Len Bullock for $2.25   Colts revolver

01.03.1863   Cloudy this morn prepared orders all day no letters this ~~morn~~ to night
Expect pay day Monday

01.04.1863   Danville Ky Rainy to-day made out accounts all day – Paymaster came and commenced paying this P.M. Paid Cos. A.B.C.&D the rest pd to morrow Cleared off very pleasant

01.05.1863   Continued Paying off – made most of the time got through about 4   no news wrote to Fred

01.06.1863   Business quite brisk no letter for me wrote to father
              for Dan Madux

01.07.1863   Very pleasant day   Business dull   no news   camp
              matters about the same   got a letter from mother &
              may & Lizzie answered it

01.08.1863   quite cold but pleasant Blake and Dan down to the
              hospitale   collecting   nothing new   getting boots
              mended to day

01.09.1863   Camp band Danville got up early Blake went to   &
              Lexington to day trade dull got box stationary no
              letter pleasant

01.10.1863   Camp Baird Rainy & cold got the things from town
              2 loads Business very brisk cleared off pleasant no
              news from home or elsewhere

01.11.1863   A "splendid day" all quiet and lonesome stopped
              in & wrote to ma Walker & Marth & read nothing
              new

01.12.1863   "Pleasant Business brisk & change plenty a wonder
              got a letter from Marth & chas. Answered it all well
              at home

01.13.1863   Danville Pleasant – Business brisk no particular war
              news Prospect dark got a letter from Arth Murse,
              Portsmouth Va. Blak went to

01.14.1863   Raines all day   Theodre Jones came from Racine
              stoped with us to night no letter – continue to storm
              stormed all night

01.15.1863   Storm continues hard with snow wind & rain things dull stormy all day mail did not come, roads obstructed.

01.16.1863   Danville – Snows hard & cold a thdy very cold no mail to night Had oysters for supper bully for them storm abated but colder slept well on our straw ground bed

01.17.1863   Morn still very cold & Wisconsinist & cloudy – business dull. No mail to night Bridges on the R R washed away cold night Ad Lytle died

01.18.1863   Pleasant & warm Wrote to Birn & went to see Jim Murphy very low and not much better Weather Comfortable Blake came

01.19.1863   Danville Ky. All well as usual cloudy this morning & cool Business quite dull mail arrived got letters from Birn Fred & all the folk at home – all well

01.20.1863   Very rainy & unpleasant & was all last night no letter Dan got one from home Lucy better & ida sick with diphera – went to see Jim getting along well rainy

01.21.1863   Cool & cloudy – Went to town with Mr Blake after the goods had not come, harnessed the team & moved our wagon to another shop for repairs got a letter from Weaver & Marth & Chas

01.22.1863   Danville – goods not yet arrived consequently business dull weather cloudy no letter to night had a game of old sledge in eve first for quit while

01.23.1863   Cloudy & dark Went down town in Eve trade dull all day Expect the goods tomorrow got letter from Jim Balding   rumors of going to Vicksburg

01.24.1863   goods come all but the apples Business very brisk all day Went to see Jim- very low & dangerous got a letter from Mose Walker all well wrote home

01.25.1863   Danville Camp Baird Ky. Went down town no more things for us Brot the wagon to camp Opened all day Business dull shall probably go to morrow ples. Weth. Went to see Jim Feels better to night rainy weather

01.26.1863   Danville & on the road Started at 8 Louisville 85 miles passed along all night rainy & cold in P M slept in the wagon & most frose   snow & rain

01.27.1863   on the march snow & rain & mud went 15 or 18 miles hard times

01.28.1863   on the march snow & cold started at 8 went to camp at 41/2 very cold slep in 2 tent

01.29.1863   On the march very cold rainy weather Regt in advance Clear but cold today Went 18 miles campd at 4

01.30.1863   on the march started early got into Louisville at 1 campd out the city got a letter from Chas wrote home slept in the wagon

01.31.1863   Louisville Ky. Did not move today went down town bot a pair of Boots at $5 quite a city slept in the wagon Learned of Cousin Ida's death

****

Appleton's entries end – Dyer's entries begin

****

ᗯ

February 1863
02.03.1863   attack on fort Donelson was re pulsed with a heavy loss Started back to Columba

ᗯ

March 1863
03.04.1863   Skirmishing near Thompson's Station Vandorn withdrew his forces

03.05.1863   Heavy fighting near Thompson's Station Killed and Captured 2500 federals victory complete

03.08.1863   Skirmishing across Harpeth near Dr S Webbs Vandorn with drew his forces and started back towards Columbia

03.24.1863   Start toward Nashville on a Scout Rode nearly all night

03.25.1863   Fighting at Brentwood captured 810 Federals wagons teams comesary

03.26.1863   Continued our travail toward Spring hill arrived there that day

03.27.1863   camp at Captain Thompsons Near Spring hill

03.28.1863   Went on an escort with the General to Columba

03.29.1863   Sunday at Columba resting

03.30.1863   Remained at Columba with the General

03.31.1863   Cold and windy went to Spring hill Skirmishing near Thompson's Station

❦

April 1863

04.01.1863   Cold and fare   in camp near Spring hill   false alarm

04.02.1863   Cold windy & Clear went on a foraging expedition

04.03.1863   The weather Continues the same went on a scout returned without action

04.04.1863   Skirmishing off the Lewisburg pike   drove the federals back to franklin Then we returned

04.05.1863   Weather fine acted as cour   Col Starnes captured 7 federals

04.06.1863   The weather Continues fine   Dull times in camp eavning drill

04.07.1863   continues fine   eavning fighting at Charleston eavning drill

04.08.1863   Continued fighting at Charleston eavning drill

04.09.1863 Grand review of Vandorn entire army the Same very imposing

04.10.1863 A Sharp fight near Douglass Church the yanks captured our batteries we recaptured them

04.11.1863 Rested and revived from our Fridays laybour

04.12.1863 Moved the other side of the pike alarm in the eavning no action

04.13.1863 Rainy dark dreary times dull General started to Thulahomer

04.14.1863 The weather continues the same nothing new in camp

04.15.1863 Times dull The weather dark & dreary

04.16.1863 The weather fine and pleasant times very dull Received a letter from home today

04.17.1863 Thimes dull The weather very fine no nuse

04.18.1863 General inspection Tents and Surplus baggage ordered to the rear Skirmish between pickets

04.19.1863 It rained to day Col Dibberell & Edmonson ordered to Florence Cleared of this Eavning

04.20.1863 general review today the weather pleasant times dull

04.21.1863 Fine weather Acted as Courer ordered to cook & keep on hand rations

04.22.1863   Fine day drill Sabre drill in the Eavning

04.23.1863   A pickett Skirmish in the morning Inspection two
              day   Drill in the Eavning

04.24.1863   Ordered to Decater   Started at 2 clock AM went to
              Colmby

04.25.1863   Sadursday I arrived at McCords 10 oclock Am went
              to Mothers stayed that night

04.26.1863   Started forth   went through Shelbyville took the
              fayete Pike stayed all night at Prossers

04.27.1863   Continued our march   stayed that night near the
              Tenn & Ala line

04.28.1863   Marched on through Athens   crossed the river at
              Brown's ferry and

04.29.1863   Traveling to overtake the command   we recrossed
              the river at Decater

04.30.1863   Remained with the wagons   sick with the flucks
              Fight at day's Gap Sand mountain

                              ⟨∿⟩

May 1863
05.01.1863   Remained near Decater   Sick with the Diarear
              caught up with the group at Blutville at fight

05.02.1863   Remained near the same place   fight near gatsden
              also that night at turkey town

1863

05.03.1863   Remained at the same place   captured the entire command 1675 and col Strait

05.04.1863   Moved to   to wate   until the return of the command

05.05.1863   Some 26 prisonors and Some Muls came in

05.06.1863   Received news of the capture of 1500 prisnors and mules

05.07.1863   Went out in the country foraging   had English peas for dinner

05.08.1863   Remained at Moresville   wating for the Return of the command

05.09.1863   Ordered across the river with the wagons to Danville

05.10.1863   Continued our march went through Danville & took the road toward Moulton

05.11.1863   Remained near Danville wating for the command to return which we learn was coming

05.12.1863   Went to Moulton and met the command greatly fatigued

05.13.1863   Moved to Athens   to rest & wate for general Forrest to return from Shelbyville

05.14.1863   Moved our camp East of Athens

05.15.1863   Remained in camp at the same place

05.16.1863   Remained in camps went to church at night

05.17.1863   The command remained at the same place

05.18.1863   Started toward Spring hill camped near Elktown

05.19.1863   Continued our march   Bivouched   for the night North of Pulaskey

05.20.1863   Arrived at Columba 10 oclock AM went a foraging

05.21.1863   Arrived at Spring hill

05.22.1863   Fireday   remained in camps resting the weather clear and very dry

05.23.1863   Sadursday no chang   went out a foraging Dry & warm

05.24.1863   Went out on a Scout Brought in some negroes who was acting as spies heavy flogging

05.25.1863   Dry and warm No news times dull

05.26.1863   Moved our camps   The news very flattering from Vicksburg

05.27.1863   The weather the same   News from Vicksburg very good

05.28.1863   Things very still in camps the news continues good from Vicksburg   I am on detale service

05.29.1863   A pleasant shower Gen Armstrong started in the direction
Of Mt. pleasant

05.30.1863   On duty it rained to day Al quiet in front News from Vicksburg good

05.31.1863   Showery & Sun Shiny All quiet in front the news from Vicksburg continues very good

∽

June 1863

6.01.1863   On duty to day quite pleasant news flattering from Vicksburg Picket fighting in front

06.02.1863   Ordered to prepare rations Rany morning went on a Scout in the Eavning Returned last night

06.03.1863   Prepared Rations and ordered to march the order countermanded we stayed & prepared four days rations

06.04.1863   Went to Franklin drove the federals on the north Side of the river went in two town returned to the reaste

06.05.1863   Friday renewed the attack Skirmished lightly foraged near Franklin & returned

06.06.1863   Ordered two prepare Five days rations & be ready two Start at five Oclock PM Started in the direction of Bathursday went 4 miles

06.07.1863   Moved to Bathursday went on a Scout a round by Eagleville down by Big spring Thence into Rutherford County in the direction of Lizard

06.08.1863   Went to Lizard Turned in the direction of Windrows thence Towards Eagleville and to Bathursday

06.09.1863   Went on a Scout had an engagement near Tryune on the Petersburg road the command returned at night

06.10.1863   Remained in camp at Bathursday to rest the command

06.11.1863   Went to Tryune had a fight on the pike near Samuel Perkins retired

06.12.1863   Moved the command to springhill to await orders clear and beautiful

06.13.1863   Remained in camp resting Gen N B Forest was Shot by Lieut Gould of Morton's battery serious but not dangerous

06.14.1863   Remained in camp on detale service no news to day

06.15.1863   Forest Generals moved to Columba to awate for the General to get well started late in the PM

06.16.1863   Remained at home went to harvesting wheat very Sultry, it Rained this eavning

06.17.1863   Harvest wheat warm & sultry

06.18.1863   Continued harvesting wheat – warm and Showery

06.19.1863   Compelted my wheat harvest

06.20.1863   Sadurday went A visiting Stayed All night at H H pate's

06.21.1863   Went to my command found it encamped at Gidion Pillow's between Columbia & Mt Pleasant

06.22.1863   Went to Columba and acted as policeman Returned to camp that evening

06.23.1863   Moved to Springhill The weather clear news good from the army

06.24.1863   Rany day times dull Gen Forrest went to Shelbyville to see Gen Bragg conserning orders yankey raid near Unionville

06.25.1863   Continued Raining news good from Vicksburg The Yanks yanks returned from Unionville to Tryune

06.26.1863   Ordered to prepare ration and be ready to move at 3 PM we started and went towards Reges X roads

06.27.1863   Continued our march went to Unionville Shelbyville turned around crossed the river below

06.28.1863   Continued our march and south During the day towards Thulahoma and arrived there that Eavning

06.29.1863   Skirmishing commenced at Thulahoma Starns wounded Several wounded heavy rains to day

06.30.1863   Ordered to the front then back to Thulahoma thence to decuard & on to cowan's depot Col Starnes died T P Dean Died

∽

July 1863

07.01.1863   Went to   from Cowan back to decard then to Pelham in Grundy Co Evacuation of Thulahoma by Gen Bragg

07.02.1863   Went from Pelham to Dekard thence to Winchester Salan and Brandyville Battle at Bethpage Bridge

07.03.1863   Went Fayetteville in Serch of wagons turned back towards Huntsville Brag retreating Skirmishing Between Cavalry daily

07.04.1863   continued our travail through new Madrid buckhorn tavern took the road towards Stephson

07.05.1863   Went up the railroad through wodville ScoBville Pikeville encamped near the foot of the mountain

07.06.1863   Went to belfont , learned the bridge was burnt across the Tenn River at Bridgeport we crossed the river at Belfont fery and encamped on the Sand mountain

07.07.1863   Took up our march towards Bridgeport over Sandmountain and up the cove my horse very lame & his back Sore running every day

07.08.1863   Started on to Bridgeport walking leading my horse stoped and had him shod passed Bridgeport took the road for Chatenoga stayed at the

07.09.1863   Thursday persued my course caught up with the command 4 miles east of Chatenoga encamped it has been raining daily for some time

07.10.1863   Encamped near chatenoga on duty to day All quiet Since the fall of Vicksburg & victory of Leay in Pensyvania

07.11.1863   Remained in camp Gen Forest went South on a furlow Capt Boon ordered to report to capt Mcdail

07.12.1863   Remained in warm and rainy

07.13.1863   All quiet no news Rains daily times very dull Soldiers much depressed the weather warm and Sultry

07.14.1863   Inspection of arms to day the news from fort Hudson bad to the South

07.15.1863   Continues to rain Discontentment continues 17 of the boys left for parts unknown

07.16.1863   Inspection of horses the captain went to bring to bring those Back that have gone moved our camp to Mcdowell

07.17.1863   Remained in camp Georgia Co. unwell to day mustered for pay

07.18.1863   times dull here fighting on the cost at Charlston & at Jackson Miss the news favorable so fare the result unknown

07.19.1863   Inspection of arms to day signed the parole times dull the yanks in North Ala At Hunstsville Athens &c

07.20.1863   On duty to day warm and Sultry Sickness in camp Time very dull
Soldiers in low Spirits

07.21.1863   warm and Sultry no move to day Some of the boys returned Several of the company Back

07.22.1863   The weather continues the same on duty to day very warm

07.23.1863   Went to Chatanoga Gen Forrest returned to his command Rote a letter to my wife

07.24.1863   Went to Chatanoga Drill to day & inspection of arms Gen Forrest denied putting us in the Elite core

07.25.1863   Remained in camp ordered to prepare four days ration and be ready to march the next morning

07.26.1863   Started towards Kingston By the way of paris Atans &c warm and Sultry & occasional Shower

07.27.1863   Continued our course passed through Georgetown Charlestown crossed Hiwassa and encamped for the night

07.28.1863   Went to Athens McMinn Co. Arrived there at 11 Oclock AM
Enemy to rest and wate for the command to come up Prepared rations

07.29.1863   Started from Athens went northwest crossed river at pinhook continued our course encamped at Rody's

07.30.1863   Went north East crossed Clint river went to Kingstown and encamped. It rained to day

07.31.1863   Travailed Southwest crossed the Holston at Louden and encamped Gen Forrest went on the cars to Knoxville

August 1863

08.01.1863   The company remained in camp I rode into the country, warm and Sultry Gen Forrest returned

08.02.1863   Went to Kingston and encamped continues very warm know news times dull

08.03.1863   On duty to day times dull Warm & Sultry we are encamped Between the church & Tenn

08.04.1863   Rode into the country, no news Times dull mustered for pay

08.05.1863   Remained in camp unloaded a boat wint in bathing daily

08.06.1863   Drawing to day drawed coat pants & Shirt Rode with the Gen on inspection Capt Boon Returned

08.07.1863   On duty to day rode into the country mustered for pay the news from France favorable

08.08.1863   Clear and beautiful drew our pay to day wrote a letter home today Every thing quiet

08.09.1863   Remained in camp no news on duty to day four of the prodigals returned

08.10.1863   Calm and Sarene no news All very quiet

08.11.1863   A perfect monotony in the times All very quiet I am becoming very restless

08.12.1863   On duty to day Received payment

08.13.1863   Remained in camp warm and Sultry no news today

08.14.1863   Nothing transpires to remove the monotony of camp life Very warm and Sultry

08.15.1863   Times continues the Same nothing new to relate we are encamp on the Clinch one mile from its mouth

08.16.1863   Continuation of the Same doing but little on duty bathing daily

08.17.1863   Warm and Sultry Nothing to Stir us to action.

08.18.1863   continuation of the same ordered to prepare four days ration order countermanded

08.19.1863   Ordered to prepare and keep on hand three days ration and be ready to Start at any time

08.20.1863   Order to be ready to Start the next morning at four AM order countermanded Heavy Cannonading at Charlston

08.21.1863   Thanksgiving day The day was set apart by President Davis for fast & prar   Ordered to Start AM

08.22.1863   Started and went to Roddys and encamped A Great deal of movement and changing of the commands

08.23.1863   Returned to Kingston very warm and dusty Reported advance of Rosecrants

08.24.1863   Remained at our old camps, awating orders

08.25.1863   continued at the Same place expecting orders Gen Forrest went to Loudon

08.26.1863   Continued at the Same place, received news of the fall of Fort Sumter Gen Forrest Returned to Loudon

08.27.1863   Remained in camp Received orders late PM to be ready to Start early the nisest morning duty to day

08.28.1863   After the usual stir and bustle we moved of in the direction of Woodville Thence toward Knoxville

08.29.1863   Reconoitered on Clinch river then turned back to Kingston and encamped

08.30.1863   Remained quiet until eavning ordered to prepare ration and be ready to march at five Oclock PM Skirmishing afternight

08.31.1863   Returned back to Kingston Sunday night Encamped next day went down the road towards Athens

ᕦᕤ

September 1863

09.01.1863 Went to Sweetwater down the railroad through mouth creek Station and Encamped for the night

09.02.1863 Continued our march down the railroad through Philadelphia Charleston &c Cannonading at Thulahoma The Bridge burned at Loudon

09.03.1863 Continued our march through Cleveland to Chatanoga dry and extremely dusty

09.04.1863 Moved our camps to the mouth of the chickahoma near Harrison Capt Roads 1st Geog Reg was Shot

09.05.1863 Remained in camp Shelling across the Tenn at Chatanoga and above there

09.06.1863 Remained quiet until twelve Oclock Then ordered to prepare rations went to Ringole

09.07.1863 Left Ringole and travailed about twenty five miles on the Road towards Rome and encamped Yanks thick in Wiles Valey

09.08.1863 Continued our travil came to the road leading from Summerville to Rome turned toward Summerville and encamped

09.09.1863 Started for the mountain, Received orders turned right about and went to Lafayett Encamped

09.10.1863 Ordered to move to Dalton Pegram engaged the enemy During the day Capturing 58 prisners

09.11.1863   Started on to Dalton ordered to Ringole with the army fought them and returned back during the day Gen Forrest was wound two of his body guard near Tunnel hill

09.12.1863   Formed in line of Battle at tunnelhill   the yanks falling Back and we persued Pegram fighting on the right

09.13.1863   Bragg forms his line of Battle, Rosa forms his heavy skirmishing in front   Remained in line of Battle during the night

09.14.1863   Went out on the front   the yanks moves of west, Armstrong skirmishing, Bragg and Rosa maneuvering considerably

09.15.1863   Went to Dalton, by the way of Ringole troops arriving here from the South A great move on hand

09.16.1863   Remained in camp to rest and cook rations It Being the first days rest in 16 day   troops continue to arrive

09.17.1863   moved to Tunnelhill   Encamped   ordered after dark, went to Ringole, Heavy skirmishing in front of Ringole

09.18.1863   Heavy Cavalry fighting   Braggs army advancing Great maneuvering of Bragg's & Rosa's army

09.19.1863   The Battle opened early with Cavalry Then with infantry which was fierce and terrific Lasting from 8 AM until 8 PM three of the escort wounded

09.20.1863   The Battle at nine AM and lasted until Seven PM which was fierce Brag advantage & holding every P

09.21.1863   Rosencrants retreating toward Chatanooga Bragg Persuing heavy Cavalry fighting

09.22.1863   Bragg advancing   Rosa fortifying at Chatanooga heavy Skirmishing Gen Forrest horse Shot

09.23.1863   Brags line of Battle closing on Chatanooga Rosa has taken his Stand and fortifying

09.24.1863   Heavy cannonading very heavy from eleven until one at night

09.25.1863   Cavalry commanded by Gen Forrest moved off to the right   Cannonading at Chatanooga, Skirmish near Cleavland captured six federals

09.26.1863   The command moved on engaged the enemy near Charleston Capturing near 75 federals and routing the command Commanded by Woodford

09.27.1863   Engaged the enemy near Athens Commanded by Woodford Capturing 60 or 70 prisners

09.28.1863   Gen Forrest back to Charlestown   He was also ordered to turnover apart of his command to Gen Wheeler

09.29.1863   Returned to Cleavland Gen Wheeler commenced crossing the Ten River

09.30.1863   Returned to the Misionary hills

༺

October 1863

10.01.1863   Ordered back to Graysville It Rained during the day. Gen Forrest went to Atlanta

10.02.1863   Went to Dalton to rest and recruit our horses a portion of the Vicksburg troops reinforcing Bragg

10.03.1863   Continued in camp   Reinforcements going to Chatanooga with seage guns Braggs army continues in line of Battle

10.04.1863   Went into the county No change in events Vicksburg troops arriving at Dalton

10.05.1863   Heavy cannonading at Chattanooga   with Seage guns Firing at the Pontontons Bridges

10.06.1863   Remained at the same place Same cannonading at Chattanooga It rained to day

10.07.1863   No Change in events worthy of notice   Some Vicksburg troops going to Bragg

10.08.1863   Went to Cleavland on detale service in the cars The weather fine and beautiful Troops going to Bragg

10.09.1863   Returned to Dalton President Davis passed Dalton en rout for Gen Bragg's Quarters

10.10.1863   Heavy cannonading near Chattanooga Rumors of Gen Forrest's resignation

10.11.1863   All quiet to day went to church

10.12.1863   Cannonading at Chattanooga Favorable news from Gen Wheeler in middle Tenn

10.13.1863   A very rainy day camps full of Rumor conserning gen Forrest resignation, and going on a privateer vessel

10.14.1863   Rumor partially confirmed by Northern papers Conserning Wheeler Captures in Middle Tenn

10.15.1863   It continued to rain three bridges washed off between Ringole and Chattanoog

10.16.1863   Received possitive assurance that gen Forrest had resigned, And was going to raise an independent command

10.17.1863   No change to day A great deal of gossip in regard to Gen Forrest intention Went to church

10.18.1863   Wet and Showers went to church All gosseping to day

10.19.1863   Stephensons division moving to the right up to Charleston Gen Forrest returned at 11 oclock

10.20.1863   No news Gen Forrest went to see Gen Bragg preparing to move Col Dibrell Captured 400 federals 6 pieces of artilery 40 or 50 wagons 6 ambulances with their camp equipment

10.21.1863   Gen Forrest returned Rany day Very disagreeable

10.22.1863   It continued to rain   The federal prisoners arrived from Philadelphi   Gen Forrest Started to Atlanta & Montgomery

10.23.1863   Wet and very disagreeable, at great deal of gosseping in regard to our future position

10.24.1863   Clear and pleasant   No news worthy of note

10.25.1863   Went to Church   wet and disagreeable

10.26.1863   Remained in camp, passing of the time By reading newspapers

10.27.1863   No Change in our Caps   Heavy cannonading at Raccoon mountain

10.28.1863   Skirmish at Raccoon mountain By Longstreet on ourside , Cheatham moving to Charlestown

10.29.1863   A great move expected to commence soon by Bragg Gen Forrest returned

10.30.1863   Gen Forrest went to the Front to consult with Gen Bragg

10.31.1863   Gen Forrest returned   Preparing for a move very soon

ᘒ

November 1863

11.01.1863   Troops passing to thr   front.   Gen Forrest went to Cleavland and returned   Preparing for a long move

11.02.1863   Started on our journey for the west went to Resacca and encamped

11.03.1863   persued   our journey slowly towards Rome and encamped

11.04.1863   Went through Rome and encamped inspection of horses arms equipage wrote a letter home Drawed equipage

11.05.1863   Started our march   went to Cave Spring and Bivouached

11.06.1863   Travailed towards Jackson ville , went about twenty miles and encamped at Ladegar, Ala

11.07.1863   Went through Jacksonville turned to the right, went about four miles and encamped Our officers under arrest

11.08.1863   persued our course   crossed the Coosa river at Greensport on detale encamped

11.09.1863   Persued our course passed through Ashville, weather very cold Heavy frost encamped

11.10.1863   Continued our course passed through Springville, The weather continues the same

11.11.1863   Continued our march   passed through Elyton Jonesboro & encamped

11.12.1863   Continued our march travailed about thirty miles and en   The weather pleasant

11.13.1863   Persued our journey passed through Tuscalosa Crossed the Big Warrior River and encamped

11.14.1863   Remained in camp to rest & Shoe our horses &c on detale

11.15.1863   Renewed our march and travailed on to Sipsy Creek and encamped for the night

11.16.1863   persued our journey passing through a poor and swampy country encamped on Coalfire Creek

11.17.1863   Continued our journey the country fertile encamped at Jimerson's Mill 8 miles north east of Columbus Miss

11.18.1863   Continued our march past through Caledonia and camped four miles from the Tombigly River country and citizens welthy

11.19.1863   Crossed the Tombigby pass through Aberdean and encamped six miles from Ocalona   The land thin farms large Monroe County

11.20.1863   persued our march passed through Oakalona Chickasaw County & encamped in the county of Pontotoc. Slight rain

11.21.1863   Remained in camp to rest seven miles from Oakalona The country rich & fertile The weather damp and cloudy

11.22.1863   Moved back to Oakolona went into camp close to town our officers released

11.23.1863   Remained in camp resting   Shoeing horse and preparing for a march A requisition for clothes

11.24.1863   Remained in camp Draw coats Pants Shirts Drawers & Shoes A rainy morning

11.25.1863   Remained in camp preparing for a march ordered to prepare four days rations and be ready to start at 8 Oclock AM

11.26.1863   Distance from Oakolona to Pontotoc   Started on our march towards Pontotoc went within six miles of there and encamped

11.27.1863   Went to Pontotoc Stored Ordinance, went into camp I went to New Albany with a dis patch   Distance 25 miles

11.28.1863   Went to New Albany encamped, I went from Albany to Pontotoc and back Lost my Pocketbook

11.29.1863   Remained in camp on account of high water   very cold yesterday and to day   Distance from Pontotoc to New Albany 20 m

11.30.1863   Remained at New Albany building a bridge across Hatchey river very cold   Prepared rations

∽

December 1863
12.01.1863   Started fro West Tennessee Gen S D Lee accompanies us went near Ripley and encamped Dis about 20 miles

12.02.1863   Persued our journey across the Tenn & Miss State line near sunset and arrived at Saulsbery about dark travail eight miles on Hardeman County Tenn The command kept their Saddles No sleep to night

12.03.1863   Started early, arrived at Bolivar   Commenced crossing the Big Hatchey in a flat Boat Completed our crossing   went to Medon arrived there about midnight

12.04.1863   Went to Jackson and encamped in Town at the Livery Stable, Having been on a march near five hundred miles

12.05.1863   Remained in Jackson A gay time with the citizens the Horses at the Livery the soldiers at the Tavern

12.06.1863   Gen Forrest went to Spring creek to inspect Col Falkner's command, And returned I went to the Episcapalian church to day

12.07.1863   No change the same rotine of duty twenty of the company detaled to go in the country to make some arrests

12.08.1863   Remained at Jackson The detale recruited Rainy day All quiet

12.09.1863   The command remained in camp went into the country to procure hands to work on a bridge

12.10.1863   Remained in Jackson Nothing transpired to remove the monotony of camp life on duty of some kind nearly every day

12.11.1863   Remained in Jackson   All quiet   wet and disagreeable

12.12.1863   Remained in Jackson, rainy and disagreeable   on duty to day

12.13.1863   Remained in camp went to the Episcopalian church Bells commenced Started to Oaklona to draw arms &c

12.14.1863   Remained at Jackson   receiving and organizing troops rapidly

12.15.1863   No change to note twenty of the company went into the country on detale and returned

12.16.1863   All quiet No change The Gen Sick very rainy to day

12.17.1863   Cold and disagreeable No change

12.18.1863   Very disagreeable Nothing to report we are going through the regular rotine of duty

12.19.1863   Remained at Jackson   The Boys makin   great preparations for a party to take place

12.20.1863   Remained at Jackson All quiet A pleasant day

12.21.1863   Went into the country on detale the pickets was Sent out for the party very pleasant

12.22.1863   Returned from the country The party was all of the talk Two yanks Brought in

12.23.1863   Ordered to prepare ration and be ready to start at a moments warning. The Great Ball came off it passed off well

12.24.1863   Started from Jackson at 4 Oclock PM Crossed the Big Hatchey at Estanaula at 11 Oclock PM Run into Yankey pickets at 12 PM Drove them 4 M

12.25.1863   Remained on the road wating for the command to cross the river Spending our Christmas day on the road wating for orders

12.26.1863   Started on our march engaged the Yankeys South of Summerville killing and capturing 40 captured four wagons One of escort killed and two wounded Gen Forrest his commission as Major gen

12.27.1863   Continued our journey passed through Macon Crossed Bar river at Lafayed , drove off the Enemy capturing their camp Equipage & commissairy destroyed railroad & wagons

12.28.1863   Travailed all night that night and the next day passing through Salem Hendersonville & arrived at Hollysprisna

12.29.1863   Started and went Southwest traveled all day and encamped The command very tired

12.30.1863   Continued our course without any thing worthy of note

12.31.1863   Persued our course came to the Tenn and the Miss railroad went down the road to Como and encamped It rained the first of the day then changed to Sleet and Snow New Year at Como very cold

January 1864

01.01.1864   New year finds me at Como Tarrola County Mississippi with the command enjoying good health But very tired from a very hard march Coming from west Tenn

01.02.1864   Remained at Como the weather extremely cold & disagreeable Snow and Sleet daily we are without tents or cooking vessels

01.03.1864   We are at the same place and no Change to relate Snow and Sleet daily without any moderation

01.04.1864   No Change to relate Gen Forrest has gone to Gen. Polk's headquarters on business No change in the weather Gen Polk is at Demoply Ala. With his army corp

01.05.1864   Remained at Como the weather remains the Same very disagreeable we are employed in unloading the cars of its Supplies almost daily

01.06.1864   Remained at Como No Change to relate We draw Pork Beef Meal and Peas & occasionally flower and potatoes

01.07.1864   Remained at Como Sleet and Snow falling nearly every day We have fixed up Camps and are living tolerably

01.08.1864   Remained at Como the Sun Shone out Some to day for the first time this year, they are some of moderation

01.09.1864   The weather is moderating Slightly though it is very cold yet

01.10.1864   Nothing new to relate we are receiving Supplies for the command daily and are chiefly employed in unloading cars

01.11.1864   Remained at Como no change

01.12.1864   Remained at Como the weather gradually moderating

01.13.1864   Remained at Como the weather becoming Pleasant

01.14.1864   Remained at Como A Beautiful day No change in the command

01.15.1863   Remained at the Same place no change

01.16.1864   Remained at Como The weather warm and beautiful

01.17.1864   At Como Gen Forrest returned to his command light rain

01.18.1864   Remained at Como Warm and beautiful A flag of truce pasing between Gen Forrest and Gen Hurlburt

01.19.1864   An exchange of prisoners affected Between Gen Forrest and Gen Hulburt I wrote a letter home to day Active preperation for the organization of the army

01.20.1864   Remained at Como A thorough reorganization of the Cavalry on foot in this command

01.21.1864   No change Drew Coats Pants Shirts Draws

01.22.1864   No Change in our affares The command very busily in organiseing, Drew Pistols, Carbeans & other equipments

01.23.1864   The weather very fine for the season Wrote a letter to my wife

01.24.1864   Remained in camp Times Dull A Drill each day

01.25.1864   Remained at Como Drew Saddles Bridles Carterages boxes &

01.26.1864   The weather fine All quiet

01.27.1864   A wagon train arrived which had been captured from the citizens who had been trading Cotton at Memphis

01.28.1864   Remained at Como Drew pay up to the first of January

01.29.1864   All quiet A drill nearly every day Gen Forrest went to see Gen Polk

01.30.1864   No Change the weather has been remarkably fine for some time the command has been very active in organising for some time

01.31.1864   Gen Forrest returned Every thing ver active man and horse in good condition orders to prepare for a march

∽

February 1864

02.01.1864   Started on our march Crossed the Hatchey at Pontotoc and encamped for the night

02.02.1864   Continued our march arrived at Oxford Lafyet County and encamped The Yankey Cavalry making Demonstrations at various places

02.03.1864   Moved to another place and went into camp near Oxford

02.04.1864   Rode into the country the weather very fine

02.05.1864   Remained at Oxford The command Drawing equipage The weather very fine

02.06.1864   Remained at Oxford Nothing new to relate

02.07.1864   Remained at Oxford the command completing of their organization

02.08.1864   Received orders to prepare rations and be ready to Start the next morning

02.09.1864   Remained in camp went to town on police duty and returned to camp at night

02.10.1864   Went on a trip after some deserters we caught them and encamped for the night

02.11.1864   Returned to Oxford Ordered to prepare and keep on hand four days rations

02.12.1864   A great talk in camp to day about Gen Forrest Shooting of Some deserter which was condemned to be Shot at 4 O clock A large Concourse of people assembled The Gen pardoned them

02.13.1864   Reported the Federals advansing in large force from Coliersville

02.14.1864   A Skirmish across the Tallahatchey near Wyatt Preparing for a move

02.15.1864   Started on our march, went South Passed through water valey and encamped at Coffeeville a very rainy night

02.16.1864   Continued our march Went to Grenada and encamped for the night

02.17.1864   Changed our course Eastward toward Starkville. Crossed   and an Passed through Bellfountain and encamped

02.18.1864   Continued our Course Cold and rainy I Saw peach blooms Arrived at Starkville went into camp

02.19.1864   Remained at Starkville Catibahay County Prepared rations

02.20.1864   Started on our march went up on the Suckeytonch A light Skirmish captured twenty one prisoners

02.21.1864   Fighting commenced at Suckeytonchy Bridge we drove them of followed them overtaken them near West Point Heavy fighting ensued We routed them J M Warren killed Lieut Holt of the escort wounded

02.22.1864   We pursued fighting commenced near Okalona we routed them pressing them heavy through the day captured six pieces of artillery 50 or 60 prisners loss on both sides Considerable Col Jeff Forrest killed Maxwell and Livingston wounded

02.23.1864   Gen Forrest sent a portion of his command in pursuit Who engaged them from Pontotoc to New Albany The Gen returned to witness the burial of his brother at Okolona he was buried with the honors of war

02.24.1864   Abandoned the pursuit Started South down the railroad traveled Slowly and encamped The command having been ordered back

02.25.1864   Went to Westpoint thence to The command Greatly fatigued Our horses in very bad condition

02.26.1864   Went to Starkville Catabahaw County and encamped Having defeated one of the largest cavalry raids of war killing and capturing a great many with all of their artillery

02.27.1864   Remained at Starkville Gen Forrest went to Columbus

02.28.1863   No change in camp Gen Forrest went to Gen Polks head quarters I went to Church

02.29.1864   Remained at Starkville all quiet in camp Drew Some equipage This ends February

∞

March 1864

03.01.1864   Wet cold and disagreeable   Remained at Starkville Recruiting our horses

03.02.1864   Remained at Starkville   Cleared of to day and the weather began to moderate

03.03.1864   No Change to relate all quiet

03.04.1864   Remained at Starkville all quiet

03.05.1864   No change going through the ordinary rotine of duty rode into the country

03.06.1864   Remained at Starkville All quiet The weather begins to assume the appearance of Spring

03.07.1864   Received marching orders and went to Columbus the same day, and encamped

03.08.1864   Remained at Columbus   expecting marching orders

03.09.1864   Remained at Columbus every thing very active in all of the departments

03.10.1864   Remained at Columbus Inspection of horses Saddles Bridles arms & etc

03.11.1864   Remained at Columbus   Great activity with the command preparing for a march

03.12.1864   Received orders to be ready to Start the next morning with five days rations

03.13.1864   The order countermanded and we remained at Columbus in readiness to march

03.14.1864   Started on our march   went to Aberdean and encamped

03.15.1864   Continued our march wet and cold through the day and encamped for the night near Carmargo

03.16.1864   Continued our march north with the Mobile and Ohio railroad and encampted at Tupelo

03.17.1864   Continued our march north with the railroad and encamped near Boonville

03.18.1864   Continued our Course Viewed the Great fortifycations at that place , the Battle field etc. Crossed the Miss and Tenn State line, And encamped in Maurry County

03.19.1864   Continued our march went through Purdy McNary County and encamped on the Jackson Road

03.20.1864   Went to Jackson and encamped our average travel being about forty miles per day

03.21.1864   Remained at Jackson resting our Stock preparing rations and etc

03.22.1864   Started north passed through Humbolt Trenton Dresden and encamped having travailed over forty miles

03.23.1864   Continued our march Crossed the Tenn & Kentucky State line near Ducktown and encamped A portion of the command under Col Falkner went to Union and captured over 500 prisoners

03.24.1864   Continued our march went through Mayfield Started Paduky Drove the federals into the fort and Gunboats captured their camps and equipage Commissary Quarter master and medical Stores Ambulances & Some 40 or 50 prisners and retired

03.25.1864   Went to Paduky with a flag of truce Returned went to Mayfield and encamped

03.26.1864   Pursued our way back passed through Ducktown Went to Dresden & encamped

03.27.1864   Pursued our Course passed through Trenton and encamped

03.28.1864   We arrived at Jackson Having averaged over forty miles per day fighting two battles capturing about 600 prisners 700 or 800 horses with various other equipage

03.29.1864   Remained at Jackson resting, and talking over our trip

03.30.1864   Received marching orders   Started on the Purdy road   turned and went through Montzumer and encamped near Pochotautas   having traveiled over fifty miles that day

03.31.1864   Went from Pochahuntas to Bolivar and encamped, Wet and Cold

∽

April 1864

04.01.1864   Re turned to Jackson Greatly fatigued

04.02.1864   Remained at Jackson resting for we were in much kneed of it

04.03.1864   Remained at Jackson everything Remarkably qyiet

04.04.1864   Remained in camp   Going through the regular rotine of camp duty

04.05.1864   Remained at Jackson Preparing for Action

04.06.1864   Nothing new to relate the departments active

04.07.1864   Received orders to cook and keep on hand four days rations and be ready to Start at any time

04.08.1864   All very quiett Quiet Cold for the Season

04.09.1864   A portion of the command moving and changing positions

04.11.1864   Started our march traveled west Passed through Brownsville Haywood County and encamped with orders to be ready to Start at two oclock Am A rainy night.

04.12.1864   We arrived at Ft. Piller and attacked the Same early in the day The Fort was defended by about 450 Blacks and 250 whites We captured about 40 Blacks & 100 Whites and killed the remainder We demolished the place

04.13.1864   After taking possession of the Commisaries and ordinance Stores and removing the Same, we Started back towards Jackson and encamped for the night near Brownsville.

04.14.1864   Continued our march and arrived at Jackson Having travailed about 140 miles in four days, Fought eight hours Killed 500 yanks and negroes cap Six pieces of artillery with all of their Stores

04.15.1864   Remained at Jackson waiting for the command to come up with all of their goods and Stores Gen Beauford went into Padukey capturing a large lot of horses

04.16.1864   Remained at Jackson Received orders to prepare rations and be ready to Start the next morning

04.17.1864   The order countermanded and we remained at Jackson Balls quite fashionable the last week I went to Episcopalian Church

04.18.1864   The command remained at Jackson Twenty of the
              Company went South as an escort to Governor I G
              Harris

04.19.1864   Talking of going South daily but we are here with a
              better prospect of Staying   Detales of the company
              going South daily

04.20.1864   Remained at Jackson   the command very busily
              getting up conscripts Deserters Horsethieves etc

04.21.1864   Remained at Jackson Daily arrival of Conscripts and
              Deserters A great many volunteering the command
              increasing rapidly

04.22.1864   Remained at Jackson Nothing new The command
              Continues in the Same business

04.23.1864   All quiet without any change   A Heavy rain in
              the P M

04.24.1864   Remained at Jackson All quiett I wint to church
              Considerable activity in the conscript department

04.25.1864   Remained at Jackson   The weather assumes the
              appearance of Spring warm and beautiful

04.26.1864   Remained at Jackson Nothing new

04.27.1864   Remained at Jackson All quiet with the exception
              of the conscrip   which is very active Eavning rides
              with ladies quite fashionable

04.28.1864   Remained at Jackson Arival of conscripts daily Some preparation for a march Balls giving nearly every night

04.29.1864   Remained at Jackson Received orders to prepare five days rations and be ready to leave on the first of May, Heavy rains

04.30.1864   Remained at Jackson Attended a Picnic Given by Miss Mollie Hubbard's School, moved to the Manass' House in consequence of a rain and went to dancing.

⁓

May 1864

05.01.1864   The order posponed and we remained on the account of heavy rains the day before The wagons and a portion of the command Started, Attended the Burial of Col. Read Went to Church

05.02.1864   Started our march Crossed the Hatchey River at Bolliver Had a light engagement with the enemy at Bolliver and then moved off Leaving two killed

05.03.1864   Continued our march South went near Bolliver and encamped

05.04.1864   Persued our course towards Tupelo Ariving within eight miles of There and encamped for the night

05.05.1864   We arrived at Tupelo Having Travailed between 40 and 50 miles per day carrying two day forage for our horse and four days ration for men

05.06.1864   Remained near Tupelo Resting and recruiting our Stock Which is in bad condition On duty two day

05.07.1864   Remained at Tupelo Nothing to relate Spent the time in entertaining of my distinguished guest

05.08.1864   Remained at Tupelo News from the Trans Mississippi Department and the army of North Virginia very good

05.09.1864   Remained at Tupelo The News from the rebel army Continues favorable

05.10.1864   Remained at Tupelo All the news favorable to the rebels

05.11.1864   Remained at Tupelo All quiett The weather warm in the day but very cold at night

05.12.1864   Remained at Tupelo The news from Virginia Dalton And the Trans Mississippi Very favorable Wrote a letter to my wife

05.13.1864   No change in camp Remained at the Same place Going through the regular rotene of Duty

05.14.1864   Remained at Tupelo A General review to day All passed of well

05.15.1864   Remained at Tupelo All quiet in camp Great Eagerness to Get the news

05.16.1864   Remained at Tupelo Great Eagerness to get the news which is quite favorable from the trans Mississippi Department Also from the Virginia Army Received orders to prepare five days rations and be ready to

05.17.1864   The order countermanded and we remained at Tupelo

05.18.1864   Remained at Tupelo The news from evry Department of the army Continues to very Chering

05.19.1864   Remained at Tupelo   Going through the regular rotene of Duty The news continues good

05.20.1864   No change of the command The news Continues favorable

05.21.1864   Remained at Tupelo No change in the command The weather warm and dry

05.22.1864   Remained at Tupelo considerable activity with the command preparing for a march

05.23.1864   Received orders to prepare for march the next day the Order countermanded and we remained at Tupelo

05.24.1864   Remained at Tupelo Received orders for thirty of the company to be ready to Start the next morning

05.25.1864   Thirty of the company went to wards riply on a Scout hunting some deserters the remainder of the company remained at Tupelo

05.26.1864   Remained at Tupelo   Going through the regular rotene of duty

05.27.1864   Remained at Tupelo   The tirty that had gone off Scouted the woods over in the neighborhood of Riply capturing fifteen deserters and returned

05.28.1864   Remained at Tupelo nothing of interest occurred

05.29.1864   Remained at Tupelo   received orders to prepare rations and be ready to move in the morning but before knight the order was countermanded

05.30.1864   Remained at Tupelo   Every thing very active Preparing for a march   News from Virginia and Georgia very exciting

05.31.1864   Remained at Tupelo Orders to be ready to start the next morning The command very active preparing for a move

⁓

June 1864

06.01.1864   Started on our march Travailed north of east went through Fulton and encamped

06.02.1864   Continued our march   Crossed the Miss and Ala State line and encamped Our average travel being about thirty five miles per day

06.03.1864   Started on our march went to Frankford received orders changing the program Our orders being countermanded we turned right about and took up our march back on the Same road

06.04.1864   Persued our course back on the Same road travailed very hard and encamped near Moresville   It has been raining every since we left Tupelo

06.05.1864   Started early and went to Tupelo for breakfast Arrived here greatly fatigyed and very mudy. Received orders to get every thing in order to Start the next morning at daylight

06.06.1864   Remained at Tupelo Resting and preparing for a march Our order for a march Suspended until the next day

06.07.1864   Started on our march went north with the railroad and encamped at Baldwin Very heavy rains and the waters high

06.08.1864   Continued our march with the railroad and encamped at Boonville It continues to rain daily

06.09.1864   Went on a reconnisancse with Gen Lee and Gen Forrest arround about Ryansa , and returned to Boonville The yanks anvansing and Gen Forrest manuvering his troops Two men from Ky shot for desertion

06.10.1864   A bout 10 oclock A m The fight began near Brice's crossroad five miles from Guntown which lasted until four in the   when we routed them We pressed them heavily, folowing them until 10 Oclock P m

06.11.1864   After resting about three hours during the night we started at one oclock over taking their rear at Big Hatchey fighting commenced we skirmished with them from their to Salam They were completely demoralized & threw away their guns and coutrements They travailed 60 miles in 24 hours

06.12.1864   We Deployed through the woods and Skirmished the woods back to riply Having in the two days past killed about 500 wounted 600 or 700   Captured 1500 Prisners Scattering the remainder in the woods Completely annihilating their 16th army core, with only 3,000 men

06.13.1864   We returned to Gunguntown 1,200 prisners arrived here to day   The command very Busily engaged catching Straglers, Bur the dead And removing captured property to this place

06.14.1864   Remained at Guntown Removing property from the Battlefield to Guntown which will require Several days Prisners Arriving and being sent to the rear

06.15.1864   Went to Tupelo to rest, It will take one week to remove the captured property Bury the dead and dispose of the prisoners Our wounded Sent to Lauderdale Spring Miss

06.16.1864   Remained at Tupelo Gen Forrest went to Columbus Miss Prisners passing down the road

06.23.1864   Found us at Tupelo Nothing of importance have transpired for several days Flags of truce going to Memphis to Consult about the Negro troops, their treatment etc.

06.24.1864   Remained at Tupelo The weather very warm and dry Every thing very dull

06.25.1864   Remained at Tupelo No change to relate The Second flag of truce Started to Memphis, Wrote a letter home to my wife

06.26.1864   All very quite the weather warm and Sultry One flag of truce returned

06.27.1864   Remained at Tupelo Nothing new to relate It continues very warm and Sultry

06.28.1864   Remained at Tupelo very warm and Sultry, The news from Ga, very encouraging All very quiett here, Flag of truce returned

06.29.1864   Remained at Tupelo Warm and Sultry Some indications of a move, The diferent departments very active Another flag of truce left here this morning which makes the 4th since the 10 inst

06.30.1864   All very quiet to day Scouts report the federals at Lagrange in heavy force, They are reparing the road from Memphis towards Corinth

ᐁᕀ

July 1864

07.01.1864   Remained at Tupelo Miss All very quiet Warm and Sultry

07.02.1864   Remained Tupelo No change to relate The Feds at Lagrange Both parties watching each others motions

07.03.1864   No change to relate All quiet went to Church Very warm

07.04.1864   Remained at Tupelo   Nothing New to relate   All quiet

07.05.1864   All quiet Remained at the Same place going through the regular rotene of Duty

07.06.1864   Remained at Tupelo   Received Orders to prepare rations and be ready to march the next morning

07.07.1864   The order Suspended and we remained at Tupelo

07.08.1864   Started on our march   went to Okolona and encamped Very warm

07.11.1864   Remained at Oklona   Every thing very active Preparing for active operations, warm and Sultry, A heavy rain

07.12.1864   Remained at Okolona until 4 P M Then Started on the Pontotoc road travailed until 11 Oclock at night and encamped within Seven miles of Pontotoc

07.13.1864   The Federals moved out from Pontotoc on the Tupelo road we commenced Skirmishing with them at Pontotoc and followed them on the Tupelo road Fighting the through the day B T Arnold wounded and died

07.14.1864   Heavy firing during the day near Harrisburg We were repulsed Also fighting on the Varrona road after night we were repulsed loss on both sides very heavy, the yanks held the Battle field The weather very warm and many   fainting

07.15.1864   Heavy Skirmishing commenced early in the morning The Federals moved off early in the morning on the Elicetown road we were pressing very close, A Forrest wounded Gen Forrest wounded in the foot

07.16.1864   Moved out with the expectation of having another fight But the Yanks moved off in the direction of Riply And we returned Gen Chalmers & Rody persuing them

0717.1864   Moved from Tupelo to Okolona, the weather extremely warm

07.18.1864   Remained at Okolono resting All quiet

07.19.1864   Remained at Okolono Nothing to relate All quiet

07.20.1864   Moved our camp to a new place Water very Scarce at Okolona

07.21.1864   Remained at Oklona in our new camps All quiet very dry

07.22.1864   Remained at Oklona All quiet

07.23.1864   Remained at Oklona All quiet Gen Forrest Started for Columbus Miss

07.24.1864   I started for Columbus Miss Pass through Merdian and encamped

07.25.1864   Continued our march and arived at Columbus at Noon Put up our horses at Lady's Stable and we remained in Town

07.26.1864   Remained in Columbus luxurateing in fruits melons etc All quiet

07.27.1864   Remained in Columbus passing off the time very pleasantly

07.28.1864   I rode into the country passing of the time very pleasantly

07.29.1864   I returned to Columbus to join the Squad that was there with the General Very warm and Sultry an occasional Shower of rain

07.30.1864   Remained at Columbus with the General Received orders to be ready to Start back to the command the next morning

07.31.1864   Started to the Command at Oklona, went to Meridian and encamped

ᐁᓴ

August 1864

08.01.1864   Continued our march and arrived at Okolona Very heavy rain

08.02.1864   Remained at Oklona Received orders to prepare for a march

08.03.1864   The order Suspended and we remained at Oklona A portion of the command went to the front

08.04.1864   Remained at Oklona   A   quiet   The command Luxurating in watermellons etc

08.05.1864   Remained at Oklona going through the regular rotene of Duty

08.06.1864   Remained at the same place Preparing for a march

08.07.1864   Remained at Oklona   received orders to prepare for a march and be ready to Start the next morning Oclock

08.08.1864   Started on our march The order Countermanded and we returned to the Same place with orders to be ready to Start the next morning at 4 Oclock A M

08.09.1864   Started on our march   went to Pontotoc, moved from Pontotoc northwest travailed twelve miles and encamped at Buttermilk Springs

08.10.1864   Pursued our journey Passing by Lafayet Springs arriving at Oxford late at night, The Enemy having evacuated the Same in the eavning

08.11.1864   Remained at Oxford Collecting and Dispersing of troops

(The diary ends here)

THE CIVIL WAR DIARY OF WILLIAM R. DYER

Edited

January 1863

01.01.1863   Danville, KY New Year in the army   Business very brisk Wrote orders all day Got a letter from Birn at *(left blank)*   Mr. Blake got here from home

01.02.1863   Pleasant day   Prepared orders for pay day all day No letters for me tonight   Traded pistols with Len Bullock for $2.25   Got a Colt revolver

01.03.1863   Cloudy this morning   Prepared orders all day   No letters tonight   Expect pay day Monday

01.04.1863   Danville, KY   Rainy today   Made out accounts all day   Paymaster came and commenced paying this P.M.   Paid Co's. A, B, C, & D. The rest will be paid tomorrow   Cleared off   Very pleasant

01.05.1863   Continued paying off   Made the most of the time Got through about 4 PM   No news   Wrote to Fred

01.06.1863   Business quite brisk   No letter for me   Wrote to father for Dan Madux

01.07.1863   Very pleasant day   Business dull   No news   Camp matters about the same   Got a letter from Mother, May, & Lizzie   Answered it

01.08.1863   Quite cold but pleasant   Blake and Dan down to the hospital collecting   Nothing new   Getting boots mended today

01.09.1863   Camp Baird - Danville   Got up early   Blake went to *(left blank)* & Lexington, KY today   Trade dull   Got a box of stationary   No letter   Pleasant

01.10.1863   Camp Baird   Rainy & cold   Got the things from town 2 loads   Business very brisk   Cleared off pleasant   No news from home or elsewhere

01.11.1863   A "splendid day"   All quiet and lonesome   Stopped in & wrote to Ma Walker & Martha & read   Nothing new

01.12.1863   Pleasant   Business brisk & change plenty   A wonder - got a letter from Martha & Charles   Answered it   All well at home

01.13.1863   Danville   Pleasant   Business brisk   No particular war news   Prospects dark   Got a letter from Arth Murse, Portsmouth, VA.   Blake went to *(left blank)*

01.14.1863   Rained all day   Theodore Jones came from [1]Racine, WI   Stopped with us tonight   No letter   Continued to storm   Stormed all night

01.15.1863   Storm continues hard with snow, wind, & rain Things dull   Stormy all day   Mail did not come Roads obstructed.

01.16.1863   Danville – Snows hard & cold all the day   Very cold No mail tonight   Had oysters for supper   Bully for them   Storm abated but colder   Slept well on our straw ground bed

01.17.1863   Morning still very cold, Wisconsinish, & cloudy Business dull.   No mail tonight   Bridges on the railroad washed away   Cold night   Ad Lytle died

01.18.1863   Pleasant & warm   Wrote to Birn & went to see Jim Murphy - very low and not much better   Weather comfortable   Blake came

01.19.1863   Danville, KY – All well as usual   Cloudy this morning & cool   Business quite dull   Mail arrived   Got letters from Birn, Fred, & all the folks at home   All well

01.20.1863   Very rainy & unpleasant & was all last night   No letter   Dan got one from home   Lucy better & Ida sick with diphtheria   Went to see Jim - getting along well   Rainy

---

1   *Appleton, a member of a Wisconsin unit, is from Highland Park, Illinois. Racine, Wisconsin is about 50 miles north of Highland Park (MapQuest, 2008)*

01.21.1863   Cool & cloudy   Went to town with Mr. Blake after the goods They had not come Harnessed the team & moved our wagon to another shop for repairs Got a letter from Weaver, Martha, & Charles

01.22.1863   Danville – Goods have not yet arrived, consequently business dull   Weather cloudy   No letter tonight Had a game of [2]Old Sledge in the evening The first for quite a while

01.23.1863   Cloudy & dark Went down town in the evening Trade dull all day Expect the goods tomorrow Got a letter from Jim Balding   Rumors of going to Vicksburg, MS

01.24.1863   Goods came - all but the apples   Business very brisk all day   Went to see Jim- very low & dangerous   Got a letter from Mose Walker   All well   Wrote home

01.25.1863   Danville - Camp Baird, Ky. Went down town No more things for us   Brought the wagon to camp Opened all day   Business dull   Shall probably go tomorrow Pleasant weather Went to see Jim - feels better tonight Rainy weather

01.26.1863   Danville & on the road Started at 8 PM   Louisville 85 miles Passed along all night Rainy & cold in the PM Slept in the wagon & almost froze Snow & rain

01.27.1863   On the march   Snow & rain & mud   Went 15 or 18 miles   Hard times

2   *Old Sledge (also known as All Fours, Seven Up, or High-Low Jack) is a card game usually played by two or four players (Wickipedia, the Free Encyclopedia, 2008)*

01.28.1863   On the march   Snow & cold   Started at 8 AM   Went to camp at 4:30 PM   Very cold   Slept two in a tent

01.29.1863   On the march   Very cold rainy weather   Regiment in advance   Clear but cold today   Went 18 miles Camped at 4 PM

01.30.1863   On the march   Started early   Got into Louisville at 1PM   Camped outside the city   Got a letter from Charles   Wrote home   Slept in the wagon

01.31.1863   Louisville, KY. Did not move today   Went down town Bought a pair of boots at $5   Quite a city   Slept in the wagon   Learned of Cousin Ida's death

****
Appleton's entries end – Dyer's entries begin
****

๑๏

February 1863

02.03.1863   Attack on Fort Donelson was repulsed with a heavy loss   Started back to Columbia, TN

๑๏

March 1863

03.04.1863   Skirmishing near Thompson's Station, TN   Van Dorn withdrew his forces

03.05.1863   Heavy fighting near Thompson's Station   Killed and captured 2,500 Federals   Victory complete

03.08.1863   Skirmishing across the Harpeth River near Dr S. Webb's   Van Dorn withdrew his forces and started back toward Columbia, TN

03.24.1863   Started toward Nashville, TN on a scout   Rode nearly all night

03.25.1863   Fighting at Brentwood, TN   Captured 810 Federal wagons, teams, and commissary

03.26.1863   Continued our travel toward Spring Hill, TN Arrived there that day

03.27.1863   Camped at Captain Thompson's near Spring Hill

03.28.1863   Went on an escort with the General to Columbia

03.29.1863   Spent Sunday at Columbia resting

03.30.1863   Remained at Columbia with the General

03.31.1863   Cold and windy   Went to Spring Hill   Skirmishing near Thompson's Station

April 1863

04.01.1863   Cold and fair   In camp near Spring Hill   False alarm

04.02.1863   Cold, windy & clear   Went on a foraging expedition

04.03.1863   The weather continues the same   Went on a scout
Returned without action

04.04.1863   Skirmishing off the Lewisburg Pike   Drove the
Federals back to Franklin - then we returned

04.05.1863   Weather fine   Acted as a courier   Colonel Starnes
captured 7 Federals

04.06.1863   The weather continues fine   Dull times in camp
Evening drill

04.07.1863   Continues fine   Evening fighting at [3]Charleston
(*SC*)   Evening drill.

04.08.1863   Continued fighting at Charleston   Evening drill

04.09.1863   Grand review of Van Dorn's entire army   The same
very imposing

04.10.1863   A Sharp fight near [4]Douglas Church   The Yanks
captured our batteries   We recaptured them

04.11.1863   Rested and revived from our Friday's labor

04.12.1863   Moved to the other side of the pike   Alarm in the
evening - no action

---

3   *There are two Charlestons in Tennessee – one in Tipton County and the*
other in Bradley County.   Dyer is nowhere near either of these, so this is
probably a reference to a Federal attack on Fort Sumter and/or Charleston,
South Carolina which occurred at this time (Tennessee Atlas & Gazetteer,
2007) (Long, 1971)

4   *Douglas Church is located near Bethesda, TN in Williamson County*
(Tennessee Atlas & Gazetteer, 2007)

04.13.1863   Rainy, dark, & dreary   Times dull   The General started to Tullahoma

04.14.1863   The weather continues the same   Nothing new in camp

04.15.1863   Times dull   The weather dark & dreary

04.16.1863   The weather fine and pleasant   Times very dull Received a letter from home today

04.17.1863   Times dull   The weather very fine   No news

04.18.1863   General inspection   Tents and surplus baggage ordered to the rear Skirmish between pickets

04.19.1863   It rained today   Colonels Dibrell & [5]James Howard Edmonson ordered to Florence, AL   Cleared off this evening

04.20.1863   General review today   The weather pleasant   Times dull

04.21.1863   Fine weather   Acted as courier   Ordered to cook & keep on hand   rations

04.22.1863   Fine day   Saber drill in the evening

04.23.1863   A picket skirmish in the morning   Inspection today Drill in the evening

04.24.1863   Ordered to Decatur, AL   Started at 2 AM   Went to Columbia

---

5   *(Allardice, 2008), p. 138*

04.25.1863   Saturday   I arrived at McCord's at 10 AM   Went to Mother's   Stayed that night

04.26.1863   Started forth   Went through Shelbyville   Took the Fayetteville Pike Stayed all night at Prosser's

04.27.1863   Continued our march   Stayed that night near the Tennessee & Alabama line

04.28.1863   Marched on through Athens, AL   Crossed the Tennessee River at Brown's Ferry and *(left blank)*

04.29.1863   Traveling to overtake the command   We recrossed the river at Decatur

04.30.1863   Remained with the wagons Sick with the flux Fight in Day's Gap at [6]Sand Mountain

∽

May 1863

05.01.1863   Remained near Decatur   Sick with the diarrhea Caught up with the group at Blountsville, AL at night

05.02.1863   Remained near the same place Fight near Gadsden, AL Also that night at Turkeytown, AL

---

6   *Sand Mountain stretches from the northwest corner of Georgia in a southwesterly direction all the way to Elyton, Alabama(present day Birmingham). Day's Gap is about fifteen miles south of Decatur, Alabama (Alabama Atlas & Gazetteer, 2006)*

05.03.1863   Remained at the same place   Captured the entire Federal command of 1,675 and Colonel Streight

05.04.1863   Moved to *(left blank)* to wait until the return of the command

05.05.1863   Some 26 prisoners and some mules came in

05.06.1863   Received news of the capture of 1,500 prisoners and mules

05.07.1863   Went out in the country foraging   Had English peas for dinner

05.08.1863   Remained at Mooresville, AL waiting for the return of the command

05.09.1863   Ordered across the river with the wagons to Danville, AL

05.10.1863   Continued our march   Went through Danville & took the road toward Moulton, AL

05.11.1863   Remained near Danville waiting for the command to return, which we learned was coming

05.12.1863   Went to Moulton and met the command, which was greatly fatigued

05.13.1863   Moved to Athens to rest & wait for General Forrest to return from Shelbyville, TN

5.14.1863   Moved our camp east of Athens

05.15.1863   Remained in camp at the same place

05.16.1863   Remained in camp   Went to church at night

05.17.1863   The command remained at the same place

05.18.1863   Started toward Spring Hill, TN   Camped near Elkton, TN

05.19.1863   Continued our march   Bivouacked for the night north of Pulaski, TN

05.20.1863   Arrived at Columbia at 10 AM   Went a'foraging

05.21.1863   Arrived at Spring Hill

05.22.1863   Friday   Remained in camp resting   The weather clear and very dry

05.23.1863   Saturday   No change   Went out a'foraging   Dry & warm

05.24.1863   Went out on a scout   Brought in some negroes who were acting as spies   Heavy flogging

05.25.1863   Dry and warm   No news   Times dull

05.26.1863   Moved our camp   The news very flattering from Vicksburg, MS

05.27.1863   The weather the same   News from Vicksburg very good

05.28.1863   Things very still in camp   The news continues good from Vicksburg   I am on detail service

05.29.1863   A pleasant shower   General Armstrong started in the direction of Mt. Pleasant, TN

05.30.1863   On duty   It rained today   All quiet in front   News from Vicksburg good

05.31.1863   Showery & sunshiny   All quiet in front   The news from Vicksburg continues very good

ᘒ

June 1863

6.01.1863   On duty today   Quite pleasant   News flattering from Vicksburg Picket fighting in front

06.02.1863   Ordered to prepare rations   Rainy morning   Went on a scout in the evening   Returned last night

06.03.1863   Prepared rations and ordered to march   The order countermanded   We stayed & prepared four days' rations

06.04.1863   Went to Franklin, TN   Drove the federals on the north side of the river   Went into town   Returned to the rest

06.05.1863   Friday   Renewed the attack   Skirmished lightly Foraged near Franklin & returned

06.06.1863   Ordered to prepare five days' rations & be ready to start at five PM Started in the direction of Bethesda, TN Went 4 miles

06.07.1863   Moved to Bethesda Went on a scout around by Eagleville, TN - down by [7]Big Springs, TN - thence into Rutherford County in the direction of Lizard *(?)*

06.08.1863   Went to Lizard Turned in the direction of Windrow, TN - thence toward Eagleville and to Bethesda

06.09.1863   Went on a scout Had an engagement near Triune, TN on the Petersburg Road The command returned at night

06.10.1863   Remained in camp at Bethesda to rest the command

06.11.1863   Went to Triune Had a fight on the pike near Samuel Perkins', then retired

06.12.1863   Moved the command to Spring Hill to await orders Clear and beautiful

06.13.1863   Remained in camp resting [8]General N B Forest was shot by Lieutenant Gould of Morton's battery Serious but not dangerous

06.14.1863   Remained in camp On detail service No news today

7   *There are seven communities in Tennessee named Big Spring or Big Springs. This one is about three miles north of Hoover's Gap (Tennessee Atlas & Gazetteer, 2007)*

8   *See Appendix III*

06.15.1863 Forrest's Generals moved to Columbia to wait for the General to get well   Started late in the PM

06.16.1863 [9]Remained at home   Went to harvesting wheat Very sultry - it rained this evening

06.17.1863 Harvested wheat   Warm & sultry

06.18.1863 Continued harvesting wheat   Warm and showery

06.19.1863 Completed my wheat harvest

06.20.1863 Saturday - Went a'visiting   Stayed all night at H.H. Pate's

06.21.1863 Went to my command   Found it encamped at Gideon Pillow's between Columbia & Mt. Pleasant

06.22.1863 Went to Columbia and acted as a policeman Returned to camp that evening

06.23.1863 Moved to Spring Hill   The weather clear   News good from the army

06.24.1863 Rainy day   Times dull   General Forrest went to Shelbyville to see General Bragg concerning orders Yankee raid near Unionville, TN

06.25.1863 Continued raining   News good from Vicksburg The Yanks returned from Unionville to Triune

---

9   *Dyer was from Eagleville, TN – eighteen miles east of Spring Hill. Evidently he went home (probably with permission) while Forrest's command experienced a pause in action due to his gunshot wound (Tennessee Atlas & Gazetteer, 2007)*

06.26.1863   Ordered to prepare rations and be ready to move at 3 PM   We started and went toward Riggs Crossroads, TN

06.27.1863   Continued our march   Went to Unionville and Shelbyville, then turned around and crossed the Duck River below

06.28.1863   Continued our march southeast during the day toward Tullahoma and arrived there that evening

06.29.1863   Skirmishing commenced at Tullahoma   Starnes wounded   Several wounded   Heavy rains today

06.30.1863   Ordered to the front, then back to Tullahoma, thence to Decherd, TN & on to Cowan, TN's depot   Col Starnes died   T P Dean Died

～

July 1863
07.01.1863   Went to *(left blank)* from Cowan, back to Decherd, then to Pelham, TN in Grundy County   Evacuation of Tullahoma by General Bragg

07.02.1863   Went from Pelham to Decherd, thence to Winchester, [10]Salem, and Branchville, TN   Battle at Bethpage Bridge

---

10   *There are five communities in Tennessee called Salem. This one, in Franklin County, is now known as Old Salem (Tennessee Atlas & Gazetteer, 2007)*

07.03.1863   Went to Fayetteville in search of wagons   Turned back toward Huntsville, AL   Bragg retreating Skirmishing between cavalry daily

07.04.1863   Continued our travel through New Market and Buckhorn Tavern, AL Took the road toward Stevenson, AL

07.05.1863   Went up the railroad through Woodville and Scottsboro to Pikeville, AL Encamped near the foot of the mountain

07.06.1863   Went to Bellefonte, AL and learned the bridge was burned across the Tennessee River at Bridgeport, AL   We crossed the river at Bellefonte Ferry and encamped on Sand Mountain

07.07.1863   Took up our march toward Bridgeport over Sand Mountain and up the cove   My horse is very lame & his back sore from running every day

07.08.1863   Started on to Bridgeport walking and leading my horse Stopped and had him shod Passed Bridgeport Took the road for Chattanooga, TN Stayed at the *(left blank)*

07.09.1863   Thursday- pursued my course and caught up with the command camped 4 miles east of Chattanooga It has been raining daily for some time

07.10.1863   Encamped near Chattanooga   On duty today   All quiet since the fall of Vicksburg, Ms & victory of Lee in Pennsylvania

07.11.1863 Remained in camp   General Forrest went south on a furlough   [11]Captain Nathaniel Boone ordered to report to Captain McDowell

07.12.1863 Remained in *(left blank)*   Warm and rainy

07.13.1863 All quiet   No news   Rains daily   Times very dull Soldiers much depressed   The weather warm and Sultry

07.14.1863 Inspection of arms today   The news from [12]Port Hudson bad for the South

07.15.1863 Continues to rain   Discontentment continues   17 of the boys left for parts unknown

07.16.1863 Inspection of horses   The Captain went to bring those back that have gone   Moved our camp to McDonald, TN

07.17.1863 Remained in camp   [13]Georgia Co.   Unwell today Mustered for pay

07.18.1863 Times dull here   Fighting on the coast at Charleston, SC & at Jackson, MS   The news favorable so far   The results unknown

---

11   *Dyer incorrectly refers to Lieutenant Boone as being a Captain. Boone did, in fact, have the responsibilities of a Captain on several occasions, though he never accepted the promotion. - (Bradley, 2006), p. 44.*

12   *On July 8th, 1863 Port Hudson, Louisiana - the last Confederate garrison on the Mississippi River surrendered following a six week siege (Long, 1971), p.381.*

13   *The ailing Dyer made a curious entry, with some reference to a Georgia Company.*

07.19.1863   Inspection of arms today   Signed the parole *(?)*
Times dull   The Yanks in North Alabama at
Huntsville, Athens, etc.

07.20.1863   On duty today Warm and sultry Sickness in camp
Time very dull Soldiers in low spirits

07.21.1863[14] Warm and sultry No move today Some of the boys
returned Several of the company back

07.22.1863   The weather continues the same   On duty today
Very warm

07.23.1863   Went to Chattanooga   General Forrest returned to
his command Wrote a letter to my wife

07.24.1863   Went to Chattanooga   Drill today & inspection of
arms   General Forrest denied putting us in the Elite
Corps *(?)*

07.25.1863   Remained in camp   Ordered to prepare four days'
ration and be ready to march the next morning

07.26.1863   Started toward Kingston, TN by way of Paris
(Harrison?) and Athens, TN, etc.   Warm and sultry
& an occasional shower

07.27.1863   Continued our course   Passed through Georgetown
and Charleston, TN   Crossed the Hiwassee River
and encamped for the night

---

14   *See Appendix IV*

07.28.1863   Went to Athens, McMinn County, TN   Arrived there at 11 AM Encamped to rest and wait for the command to come up   Prepared rations

07.29.1863   Started from Athens - went northwest   Crossed the river at [15]Pinhook Continued our course   Encamped at Roddy, TN

07.30.1863   Went northeast   Crossed the Clinch River   Went to Kingston and encamped. It rained today

07.31.1863   Traveled southwest (**should be southeast**)   Crossed the Holston River at Loudon, TN and encamped General Forrest went [16]on the cars to Knoxville, TN

〜

August 1863
08.01.1863   The company remained in camp   I rode into the country - warm and sultry   General Forrest returned

08.02.1863   Went to Kingston and encamped   Continues very warm   No news Times dull

08.03.1863   On duty today   Times dull   Warm & Sultry We are encamped between the Clinch & Tennessee Rivers

---

15   *There are two communities in Tennessee known as Pinhook, but neither fits into the route Dyer describes. It may be that there was another Pinhook which is now covered by Watts Bar Lake (Tennessee Atlas & Gazetteer, 2007)*

16   *Traveling by train was then known as traveling "on the cars".*

08.04.1863   Rode into the country   No news   Times dull
Mustered for pay

08.05.1863   Remained in camp   Unloaded a boat   Went in
[17]bathing daily

08.06.1863   Drawing today Drew coat, pants, & shirt Rode with
the General on inspection   Captain (*Lt.*) Boone
returned

08.07.1863   On duty today Rode into the country Mustered for
pay   The news from France favorable

08.08.1863   Clear and beautiful   Drew our pay today   Wrote a
letter home today Everything quiet

08.09.1863   Remained in camp No news On duty today Four
of the prodigals returned

08.10.1863   Calm and serene   No news   All very quiet

08.11.1863   A perfect monotony in the times   All very quiet
I am becoming very restless

08.12.1863   On duty today   Received payment

08.13.1863   Remained in camp   Warm and sultry   No news
today

08.14.1863   Nothing transpires to remove the monotony of camp
life   Very warm and sultry

---

17   *The "bathing" referred to by Dyer is what we would call swimming.*

08.15.1863   Times continue the same Nothing new to relate We are encamped on the Clinch River one mile from it's mouth

08.16.1863   Continuation of the same Doing but little On duty Bathing daily

08.17.1863   Warm and sultry   Nothing to stir us to action.

08.18.1863   Continuation of the same Ordered to prepare four days' rations Order countermanded

08.19.1863   Ordered to prepare and keep on hand three days rations and be ready to start at any time

08.20.1863   Order to be ready to start the next morning at four AM Order countermanded Heavy cannonading at Charleston

08.21.1863   Thanksgiving Day The day was set apart by President Davis for fasting & prayer Ordered to start AM

08.22.1863   Started and went to Roddy and encamped A Great deal of movement and changing of the commands

08.23.1863   Returned to Kingston   Very warm and dusty Reported advance of Rosecrans

08.24.1863   Remained at our old camps awaiting orders

08.25.1863   Continued at the same place   Expecting orders General Forrest went to Loudon

08.26.1863[18] Continued at the same place   Received news of the
fall of Fort Sumter   Gen Forrest returned from
Loudon

08.27.1863   Remained in camp   Received orders late PM to
be ready to start early the next morning   On duty
today

08.28.1863   After the usual stir and bustle we moved off in the
direction of [19]Woodville, thence toward Knoxville

08.29.1863   Reconnoitered on Clinch River then turned back to
Kingston and encamped

08.30.1863   Remained quiet until evening   Ordered to prepare
rations and be ready to march at five PM Skirmishing
after nightfall

08.31.1863   Returned to Kingston on Sunday night   Encamped
the next day   Went down the road toward Athens

༄

September 1863

09.01.1863   Went to Sweetwater, TN and down the railroad
through [20]Mouse Creek Station and encamped for
the night

18 *See Appendix IV*
19 *There are two communities in West Tennessee known as Woodville. Dyer may
be referring to Wood, Tennessee, which is about ten miles south of Sweetwater
(Tennessee Atlas & Gazetteer, 2007)*
20 *Mouse Creek Station is present day Niota, Tennessee. (Tennessee Atlas &
Gazetteer, 2007)*

09.02.1863   Continued our march down the railroad through Philadelphia and Charleston, TN, etc. Cannonading at Tullahoma, TN The Bridge burned at Loudon, TN[21]

9.03.1863   Continued our march through Cleveland to Chattanooga, TN Dry and extremely dusty

09.04.1863   Moved our camps to the mouth of Chickamauga Creek near Harrison, TN [22]Captain Rhodes of the 1st Georgia Regiment was shot

09.05.1863   Remained in camp Shelling across the Tennessee River at Chattanooga and above there

09.06.1863   Remained quiet until twelve o'clock - then ordered to prepare rations Went to Ringgold, GA

09.07.1863   Left Ringgold and traveled about twenty five miles on the Road toward Rome, GA and encamped Yanks thick in Wiles Valley (?)

09.08.1863   Continued our travel Came to the road leading from Summerville, GA to Rome Turned toward Summerville and encamped

09.09.1863   Started for the mountain Received orders - turned right about and went to La Fayette, GA and encamped

21   *Travelling along the railroad, Dyer has access to news from distant places via telegraph.*

22   *On September 4th in Chattanooga, Tennessee Captain Jazeb R Rhodes, Company C, 1st Confederate Regiment Georgia Volunteers was executed by a firing squad for having encouraged men of his own command to desert and receiving men as substitutes, knowing them to belong to the service, and then discharging them for a bonus (Richmond Examiner, 1863)*

09.10.1863   Ordered to move to Dalton, GA   Pegram engaged the enemy during the day capturing 58 prisoners

09.11.1863   Started on to Dalton   Ordered to Ringgold with the army   Fought there and returned to Dalton during the day   [23]General Forrest was wounded as were two of his body guard near Tunnel Hill, GA

09.12.1863   Formed in line of battle at Tunnel Hill   The Yanks fell back and we pursued   Pegram fighting on the right

09.13.1863   Bragg forms his line of Battle   Rosecrans forms his Heavy skirmishing in front   Remained in line of battle during the night

09.14.1863   Went out on the front   The yanks moved off to the west   Armstrong skirmishing   Bragg and Rosecrans maneuvering considerably

09.15.1863   Went to Dalton by way of Ringgold   Troops arriving here from the South   A great move on hand

09.16.1863   Remained in camp to rest and cook rations, it being the first day's rest in 16 days   Troops continue to arrive

09.17.1863   Moved to Tunnel Hill and encamped   Ordered after dark to Ringgold Heavy skirmishing in front of Ringgold

09.18.1863   Heavy cavalry fighting   Bragg's army advancing   Great maneuvering of Bragg's & Rosecrans's armies

23 *"Faint from pain and loss of blood he took a drink of whiskey at the surgeon's urging and did not leave the field"* (Welsh, 1995) p. 71

09.19.1863   The [24]battle opened early with cavalry then with infantry which was fierce and terrific, lasting from 8 AM until 8 PM   Three of the escort wounded

09.20.1863   The Battle, which was fierce, resumed at nine AM and lasted until seven PM   Bragg has the advantage & is holding every position

09.21.1863   Rosecrans is retreating toward Chattanooga   Bragg pursuing   Heavy cavalry fighting

09.22.1863   Bragg advancing Rosecrans fortifying at Chattanooga Heavy skirmishing   General Forrest's horse shot

09.23.1863   Bragg's line of battle closing on Chattanooga Rosecrans has taken his stand and is fortifying

09.24.1863   Heavy cannonading   Very heavy from eleven PM until one AM

09.25.1863   Cavalry commanded by Gen Forrest moved off to the right   Cannonading at Chattanooga   Skirmish Cleveland   Captured six Federals

09.26.1863   The command moved on and engaged the enemy near Charleston,   capturing almost 75 Federals and routing Woodford's command

09.27.1863   Engaged Woodford's command again near Athens capturing 60 or 70 prisoners

---

24   *Dyer is referring to the Battle of Chickamauga, the largest engagement in which Forrest's command ever fought. (Bradley, 2006) p. 83.*

09.28.1863   General Forrest went back to Charleston   He was also ordered to turn over a part of his command to General Wheeler

09.29.1863   Returned to Cleveland General Wheeler commenced crossing the Tennessee River

09.30.1863   Returned to Missionary Ridge

∾

October 1863

10.01.1863   Ordered back to Graysville, GA It rained during the day. [25]General Forrest went to Atlanta, GA

10.02.1863   Went to Dalton to rest and recruit our horses   A portion of the Vicksburg troops reinforcing Bragg

10.03.1863   Continued in camp   Reinforcements going to Chattanooga with siege guns Bragg's army continues in line of battle

10.04.1863   Went into the country   No change in events Vicksburg troops arriving at Dalton

10.05.1863   Heavy cannonading at Chattanooga with siege guns firing at the pontoon bridges

10.06.1863   Remained at the same place Some cannonading at Chattanooga It rained to day

---

25 *Dyer is mistaken as to Forrest's destination. General Forrest is taking a ten day leave of absence to visit his wife at LaGrange, Georgia (Jordan, 1868)*

10.07.1863   No Change in events worthy of notice   Some Vicksburg troops going to Bragg

10.08.1863   Went to Cleveland On detail service in the cars The weather fine and beautiful Troops going to Bragg

10.09.1863   Returned to Dalton   President Davis passed Dalton en route for General Bragg's headquarters

10.10.1863   Heavy cannonading near Chattanooga   Rumors of General Forrest's resignation

10.11.1863   All quiet today Went to church

10.12.1863   Cannonading at Chattanooga Favorable news from General Wheeler in Middle Tennessee

10.13.1863   A very rainy day Camp full of rumors concerning General Forrest's resignation and going on a privateer vessel

10.14.1863   Rumor partially confirmed by Northern papers concerning Wheeler captures in Middle Tennessee

10.15.1863   It continues to rain   Three bridges washed out between Ringgold and Chattanooga

10.16.1863   Received positive assurance that General Forrest had resigned and was going to raise an independent command

10.17.1863   No change today A great deal of gossip in regard to General Forrest's intentions Went to church

10.18.1863   Wet and showers Went to church All gossiping today

10.19.1863   Stevenson's division moving to the right up to Charleston   General Forrest returned at 11 o'clock

10.20.1863   No news   General Forrest went to see General Bragg   Preparing to move   Colonel Dibrell captured 400 Federals, 6 pieces of artillery, 40 or 50 wagons, and 6 ambulances with their camp equipment

10.21.1863   General Forrest returned   Rainy day   Very disagreeable

10.22.1863   It continued to rain   The Federal prisoners arrived from Philadelphia   General Forrest started to Atlanta & Montgomery, AL[26]

10.23.1863   Wet and very disagreeable   A great deal of gossiping in regard to our future position

10.24.1863   Clear and pleasant   No news worthy of note

10.25.1863   Went to church   Wet and disagreeable

10.26.1863   Remained in camp   Passing the time by reading newspapers

10.27.1863   No change in our camp   Heavy cannonading at Raccoon mountain

---

26   *At the invitation of Confederate President Jefferson Davis, Forrest met him in Montgomery, Alabama and accompanied him on the train from Montgomery to Atlanta, GA.   Upon reaching Atlanta, Davis wrote to General Bragg approving Forrest's transfer west and mentioning that Forrest wanted a few of his present troops to go with him to raise a new command. - (Hurst, 1993), pp. 141-142.*

10.28.1863[27] Skirmish at Raccoon Mountain by Longstreet on our side   Cheatham moving to Charleston

10.29.1863 A great move expected to commence soon by Bragg General Forrest returned

10.30.1863[28] General Forrest went to the front to consult with General Bragg

10.31.1863 Gen Forrest returned   Preparing for a move very soon

∽

November 1863

11.01.1863 Troops passing to the front. General Forrest went to Cleveland and returned   Preparing for a long move

11.02.1863 Started on our journey for the west   Went to Resaca, GA and encamped

11.03.1863 Pursued our journey slowly toward Rome, GA and encamped

11.04.1863 Went through Rome and encamped   Inspection of horses, arms,and equipage   Wrote a letter home Drew equipage

11.05.1863 Started our march   Went to Cave Spring, GA and bivouacked

27 *See Appendix IV*
28 *See Appendix IV*

11.06.1863   Traveled toward Jacksonville, AL about twenty miles and encamped at Tredegar, Ala

11.07.1863   Went through Jacksonville, turned to the right, then went about four miles and encamped [29]Our officers under arrest

11.08.1863   Pursued our course   Crossed the Coosa River at [30]Greensport, AL   On detail   Encamped

11.09.1863   Pursued our course   Passed through Ashville, AL Weather very cold Heavy frost   Encamped

11.10.1863   Continued our course   Passed through Springville, AL The weather continues the same

11.11.1863   Continued our march   Passed through [31]Elyton and [32]Jonesboro, AL & encamped

11.12.1863   Continued our march   Traveled about thirty miles and encamped The weather pleasant

11.13.1863   Pursued our journey Passed through Tuscaloosa, AL Crossed the Black Warrior River and encamped

---

29   *See Appendix V*

30   *Greensport, Alabama was evidently covered by water when the construction of a dam on the Coosa River created H. Neely Henry Lake (Alabama Atlas & Gazetteer, 2006)*

31   *Elyton is present day Birmingham, Alabama.*

32   *The Jonesboro Dyer refers to is now known as Old Jonesboro, Alabama. It is located on the western edge of Bessemer, Alabama (Alabama Atlas & Gazetteer, 2006)*

11.14.1863[33]   Remained in camp to rest & shoe our horses, etc. On detail

11.15.1863   Renewed our march and traveled on to the Sipsey River and encamped for the night

11.16.1863   Pursued our journey passing through a poor and swampy country   Encamped on Coal Fire Creek

11.17.1863   Continued our journey   The country fertile Encamped at Jimerson's Mill (?), 8 miles northeast of Columbus, MS

11.18.1863   Continued our march   Passed through Caledonia, MS and camped four miles from the Tombigbee River   Country and citizens wealthy

11.19.1863   Crossed the Tombigbee River   Passed through Aberdeen, MS and encamped six miles from Okolona, MS   The land thin   Farms large   Monroe County

11.20.1863   Pursued our march   Passed through Okolona, Chickasaw County & encamped in the county of Pontotoc.   Slight rain

11.21.1863   Remained in camp to rest seven miles from Okolona The country rich & fertile   The weather damp and cloudy

11.22.1863   Moved back to Okolona and went into camp close to town   [34]Our officers released

---

33   *See Appendix IV*
34   *See Appendix V*

11.23.1863   Remained in camp resting, shoeing horses, and preparing for a march   A requisition for clothes

11.24.1863   Remained in camp   Drew coats, pants, shirts, drawers, & shoes A rainy morning

11.25.1863   Remained in camp preparing for a march   Ordered to prepare four days' rations and be ready to start at 8 AM

11.26.1863   Distance from Okolona to Pontotoc, MS *(?)* Started on our march towards Pontotoc   Went within six miles of there and encamped

11.27.1863   Went to Pontotoc   Stored ordinance and went into camp   I went to New Albany, MS with a dispatch, a distance of 25 miles

11.28.1863   The command moved to New Albany and encamped I went from New Albany to Pontotoc and back   Lost my pocketbook[35]

11.29.1863   Remained in camp on account of high water   Very cold yesterday and today   Distance from Pontotoc to New Albany 20 miles

11.30.1863   Remained at New Albany building a bridge across the Little Tallahatchie River   Very cold   Prepared rations

ᕲᕬ

---

35   *Dyer's "pocketbook" was what we would call a wallet today.*

December 1863

12.01.1863   Started for West Tennessee   General S D Lee accompanies us Went near Ripley, MS and encamped Distance about 20 miles

12.02.1863   Pursued our journey crossing the Tennessee & Mississippi state line near sunset and arrived at Saulsbury, TN about dark   Traveled eight miles on into Hardeman County, Tennessee The command kept their saddles No sleep tonight

12.03.1863   Started early Arrived at Bolivar, TN   Commenced crossing the Hatchie River in a flat boat   Completed our crossing   Went to Medon, TN   Arrived there about midnight

12.04.1863   Went to Jackson, TN and encamped in town at the livery stable, having been on a march of nearly five hundred miles

12.05.1863   Remained in Jackson   A gay time with the citizens The horses at the livery - the soldiers at the tavern

12.06.1863   General Forrest went to [36]Spring Creek, TN to inspect Colonel Faulkner's command and returned I went to the Episcopalian church today

12.07.1863   No change   The same routine of duty   Twenty of the company detailed to go into the country to make some arrests

12.08.1863   Remained at Jackson   The detail recruited   Rainy day   All quiet

36   *There are six communities in Tennessee known as Spring Creek. This one is near the northeast corner of Madison County (Tennessee Atlas & Gazetteer, 2007)*

12.09.1863   The command remained in camp   Went into the country to procure hands to work on a bridge

12.10.1863   Remained in Jackson   Nothing transpired to remove the monotony of camp life   On duty of some kind nearly every day

12.11.1863   Remained in Jackson   All quiet   Wet and disagreeable

12.12.1863   Remained in Jackson   Rainy and disagreeable   On duty today

12.13.1863   Remained in camp   Went to the Episcopalian church   Balls[37] commenced   Started to Okolona to draw arms, etc.

12.14.1863   Remained at Jackson   Receiving and organizing troops rapidly

12.15.1863   No change to note   Twenty of the company went into the country on detail and returned

12.16.1863   All quiet   No change   The General Sick   Very rainy today

12.17.1863   Cold and disagreeable   No change

12.18.1863   Very disagreeable   Nothing to report   We are going through the regular routine of duty

12.19.1863[38]   Remained at Jackson   The boys making great preparations for a party to take place

---

37   *Parties of the holiday season.*
38   *See Appendix IV*

12.20.1863   Remained at Jackson   All quiet   A pleasant day

12.21.1863   Went into the country on detail   The pickets were
              sent out for the party   Very pleasant

12.22.1863   Returned from the country   The party was all of the
              talk   Two yanks brought in

12.23.1863   Ordered to prepare rations and be ready to start at
              a moment's warning.   The Great Ball came off   It
              passed off well

12.24.1863   Started from Jackson at 4 PM   Crossed the Hatchie at
              [39]Estanaula, TN at 11 PM   Ran into Yankee pickets
              at 12 PM and drove them 4 miles

12.25.1863   Remained on the road waiting for the command to
              cross the river Spending our Christmas day on the
              road   Waiting for orders

12.26.1863   Started on our march   Engaged the Yankees south
              of Somerville, TN killing and capturing 40 Captured
              four wagons   One of the Escort killed[40] and two
              wounded   General Forrest received his commission
              as a Major General

---

39 Estanaula, Tennessee no longer exists. In 1863 it was in Madison County
    It's location is now in Haywood County, Tennessee just northeast of Hillville,
    Tennessee across the Hatchie River. Forrest's command used the ferry there to
    make the crossing (Tennessee Atlas & Gazetteer, 2007)
40 This may have been Alfred H. (Doc) Boone, although the date of death in Dr.
    Bradley's book is 12.03.1863 (Bradley, 2006)

12.27.1863   Continued our journey Passed through Macon, TN Crossed the [41]Bar River at [42]Lafayed, TN and drove off the enemy capturing their camp equipage & commissary Destroyed railroad & wagons

12.28.1863   Traveled all night that night and the next day, passing through [43]Salem, and [44]Hendersonville, *MS* Arrived at Holly Springs, MS

12.29.1863   Started and went southwest Traveled all day and encamped The command very tired

12.30.1863   Continued our course without anything worthy of note

12.31.1863   Pursued our course Came to the [45]Tennessee and the Mississippi Railroad Went down the road to Como, Ms and encamped It rained the first of the day, then changed to sleet and snow New Year at Como Very cold

❦

41   *Dyer mistakenly calls the Wolf River the Bar (Bear) River (Tennessee Atlas & Gazetteer, 2007)*

42   *Fayette Station (Dyer calls it Lafayed) is present day Rossville, TN (Tennessee Atlas & Gazetteer, 2007)*

43   *There are four communities in Mississippi known as Salem – none of which fit Dyer's route from Rossville, Tennessee to Holly Springs, Mississippi. An 1864 map of Mississippi, however, shows there was a town of Salem just south of Spring Hill, Mississippi which fits the trip perfectly (Mississippi Atlas & Gazetteer, 2007)*

44   *There was once a Hendersonville in Yalobusha County, Mississippi, but it too doesn't fit the route Dyer describes. It is quite possible that Dyer errs by hearing and writing" Hendersonville" for Hudsonville, Mississippi. Once again, Hudsonville fits the trip (Mississippi Atlas & Gazetteer, 2007)*

45   *This was the New Orleans and Memphis Railroad.*

January 1864

01.01.1864 The new year finds me at Como in Panola County, Mississippi with the command enjoying good health, but very tired from a very hard march from west Tennessee

01.02.1864 Remained at Como   The weather extremely cold & disagreeable   Snow and sleet daily   We are without tents or cooking vessels

01.03.1864 We are at the same place and no change to relate Snow and sleet daily without any moderation

01.04.1864 No Change to relate   General Forrest has gone to General Polk's headquarters on business   No change in the weather   General Polk is at Demopolis, AL with his army corps

01.05.1864 Remained at Como   The weather remains the same - very disagreeable   We are employed in unloading the cars of supplies almost daily

01.06.1864 Remained at Como   No Change to relate   We draw pork, beef, meal, peas, & occasionally flour and potatoes

01.07.1864 Remained at Como   Sleet and snow falling nearly every day   We have fixed up camps and are living tolerably

01.08.1864 Remained at Como   The sun shone out some today for the first time this year   There are some signs of moderation

01.09.1864   The weather is moderating slightly, though it is very cold yet

01.10.1864   Nothing new to relate   We are receiving supplies for the command daily and are chiefly employed in unloading cars

01.11.1864   Remained at Como   No change

01.12.1864   Remained at Como   The weather gradually moderating

01.13.1864   Remained at Como   The weather becoming pleasant

01.14.1864   Remained at Como   A Beautiful day   No change in the command

01.15.1864   Remained at the same place   No change

01.16.1864   Remained at Como   The weather warm and beautiful

01.17.1864   At Como   General Forrest returned to his command Light rain

01.18.1864   Remained at Como   Warm and beautiful   A flag of truce passing between General Forrest and General Hurlburt

01.19.1864   An exchange of prisoners was affected between General Forrest and General Hurlburt   I wrote a letter home today   Active preparation for the organization of the army

01.20.1864   Remained at Como   A thorough reorganization of the cavalry is afoot in this command

01.21.1864   No change   Drew coats, pants, shirts, and drawers

01.22.1864   No Change in our affairs   The command is very busy organizing   Drew pistols, Carbines, & other equipment

01.23.1864   The weather very fine for the season   Wrote a letter to my wife

01.24.1864   Remained in camp   Times Dull   A drill each day

01.25.1864[46]   Remained at Como   Drew saddles, bridles, cartridge boxes, & *(left blank)*

01.26.1864   The weather fine   All quiet

01.27.1864   A wagon train arrived which had been captured from the citizens who had been trading cotton at Memphis

01.28.1864   Remained at Como   Drew pay up to the first of January

01.29.1864   All quiet   A drill nearly every day   General Forrest went to see General Polk

01.30.1864   No Change   The weather has been remarkably fine for some time   The command has been very active in organizing for some time

---

46   See Appendix IV

01.31.1864   General Forrest returned   Everything very active Man and horse in good condition Orders to prepare for a march

∾

February 1864

02.01.1864[47] Started on our march   Crossed the Hatchie River at Pontotoc, Ms and encamped for the night

02.02.1864   Continued our march   Arrived at Oxford, Lafayette County, MS and encamped   The Yankee cavalry making demonstrations at various places

02.03.1864   Moved to another place and went into camp near Oxford

02.04.1864   Rode into the country The weather very fine

02.05.1864   Remained at Oxford   The command drawing equipment The weather very fine

02.06.1864   Remained at Oxford   Nothing new to relate

02.07.1864   Remained at Oxford   The command completing their organization

02.08.1864   Received orders to prepare rations and be ready to start the next morning

02.09.1864   Remained in camp   Went to town on police duty and returned to camp at night

----

47   *See Appendix IV*

02.10.1864   Went on a trip after some deserters   We caught them and encamped for the night

02.11.1864   Returned to Oxford   Ordered to prepare and keep on hand four days rations

02.12.1864   [48]A great talk in camp today about General Forrest shooting some deserters which were condemned to be shot at 4 o'clock   A large concourse of people assembled   The General pardoned them

02.13.1864   Reported that the Federals are advancing in large force from Collierville, TN

02.14.1864   A skirmish across the Tallahatchie River near Wyatt, MS   Preparing for a move

02.15.1864   Started on our march   Went south   Passed through Water Valley, MS and encamped at Coffeeville, MS   A very rainy night

02.16.1864   Continued our march   Went to Grenada, MS and encamped for the night

48   *Nineteen deserters had been captured and brought in. Forrest sentenced them to be shot. "Their coffins were made, their graves dug, and the culprits advised to make their peace with their Maker and the world." The prisoners were seated on their coffins and Bell's Brigade was assembled to witness the executions. "All things being now ready the commanding officer said, "Present arms, make ready, take aim" – just at that moment (and before the next command, which would have been "Fire," was given) a staff officer came dashing up and said, addressing the culprits: "General Forresi has requested me to say to you that it was unpleasant to him to shed blood in this manner, and that, through the petitions of the clergy, the prominent citizens and ladies of Oxford, and your officers, if you will now promise to make good and faithful soldiers he would pardon you." They shouted: "We will ! We will !" (Hancock, 1887) pp. 309-310*

02.17.1864   Changed our course to eastward toward Starkville, MS Crossed *(left blank)* and *(left blank)* and passed through Bellefontaine, MS and encamped

02.18.1864   Continued our course Cold and rainy I saw peach blooms Arrived at Starkville, MS Went into camp

02.19.1864   Remained at Starkville in Okitibbeha County Prepared rations

02.20.1864   Started on our march Went up on the Chuquatonchee A light skirmish Captured twenty-one prisoners

02.21.1864   Fighting commenced at Chuquatonchee Bridge We drove them off, then followed and overtook them near West Point, MS Heavy fighting ensued We routed them [49]James M Warren was killed and Lieutenant Joshua Holt of the escort was wounded

02.22.1864   We pursued and fighting commenced near Okolona, MS We routed them, pressing them heavy through the day Captured six pieces of artillery, and 50 or 60 prisoners Loss on both sides was considerable Colonel Jeffrey Forrest was killed R.H. Maxwell and W.H. Livingston were wounded[50]

02.23.1864   General Forrest sent a portion of his command in pursuit, which engaged them from Pontotoc to New Albany The General returned to witness the burial of his brother at Okolona He was buried with the honors of war

---

49   *(Bradley, 2006), p. 174.*
50   *(Bradley, 2006), p. 203.*

02.24.1864   Abandoned the pursuit and started south down the railroad   Traveled slowly and encamped, the command having been ordered back

02.25.1864   Went to West Point thence to *(left blank)*   The command greatly fatigued   Our horses in very bad condition

02.26.1864   Went to Starkville, Okitibbeha County, Ms and encamped, having defeated one of the largest cavalry raids of the war, killing and capturing a great many with all of their artillery

02.27.1864   Remained at Starkville   General Forrest went to Columbus, MS

02.28.1863   No change in camp General Forrest went to General Polk's headquarters   I went to Church

02.29.1864   Remained at Starkville   All quiet in camp   Drew some equipment This ends February

∽

March 1864

03.01.1864   Wet, cold, and disagreeable   Remained at Starkville recruiting our horses

03.02.1864   Remained at Starkville   Cleared off today and the weather began to moderate

03.03.1864   No Change to relate   All quiet

03.04.1864   Remained at Starkville   All quiet

03.05.1864   No change   Going through the ordinary routine of duty   Rode into the country

03.06.1864   Remained at Starkville All quiet The weather begins to assume the appearance of spring

03.07.1864   Received marching orders and went to Columbus the same day and encamped

03.08.1864   Remained at Columbus   Expecting marching orders

03.09.1864   Remained at Columbus   Everything very active in all of the departments

03.10.1864   Remained at Columbus   Inspection of horses, saddles, bridles, arms, etc.

03.11.1864   Remained at Columbus   Great activity with the command preparing for a march

03.12.1864   Received orders to be ready to start the next morning with five days' rations

03.13.1864   The order countermanded and we remained at Columbus in readiness to march

03.14.1864   Started on our march   Went to Aberdeen, MS and encamped

03.15.1864   Continued our march   Wet and cold through the day Encamped for the night near [51]Camargo, MS

---

51   *Camargo was located in Monroe County, about a mile southwest of Nettleton, Mississippi* (Mississippi Atlas & Gazetteer, 2007)

03.16.1864 Continued our march north along the Mobile and Ohio railroad and encamped at Tupelo, MS

03.17.1864 Continued our march north along the railroad and encamped near Booneville, MS

03.18.1864 Continued our course Viewed the great fortifications at that place *(Corinth, MS),* the battlefield, etc. Crossed the Mississippi and Tennessee state line and encamped in McNairy County, TN

03.19.1864 Continued our march Went through Purdy, TN in McNairy County and encamped on the Jackson Road

03.20.1864 Went to Jackson , TN and encamped, our average travel being about forty miles per day

03.21.1864 Remained at Jackson resting our stock, preparing rations, etc.

03.22.1864 Started north Passed through Humboldt, Trenton, and Dresden, TN and encamped, having traveled over forty miles

03.23.1864 Continued our march Crossed the Tennessee & Kentucky state line near Dukedom, TN and encamped A portion of the command under Colonel W.W. Faulkner went to Union City, TN and captured over 500 prisoners

03.24.1864   Continued our march   Went through Mayfield, KY and started for Paducah, KY   Drove the Federals into the fort under the protection of their gunboats Captured their camps and equipment, commissary, quarter master and medical stores, ambulances, & some 40 or 50 prisoners and retired

03.25.1864   Went to Paducah with a flag of truce   Returned and went to Mayfield and encamped

03.26.1864   Pursued our way back   Passed through Dukedom Went to Dresden, TN & encamped

03.27.1864   Pursued our course   Passed through Trenton, TN and encamped

03.28.1864   We arrived at Jackson , TN, having averaged over forty miles per day,   fought two battles, captured about 600 prisoners and 700 or 800 horses with various other equipment

03.29.1864   Remained at Jackson resting and talking over our trip

03.30.1864   Received marching orders   Started on the Purdy Road then turned and went through Montezuma, TN and encamped near Pocahontas, TN,   having traveled over fifty miles that day

03.31.1864   Went from Pocahontas to Bolivar, TN and encamped Wet and cold

෴

April 1864

04.01.1864   Returned to Jackson, TN   Greatly fatigued

04.02.1864   Remained at Jackson resting, for we were in much need of it

04.03.1864   Remained at Jackson   Everything remarkably quiet

04.04.1864   Remained in camp   Going through the regular routine of camp duty

04.05.1864   Remained at Jackson   Preparing for action

04.06.1864   Nothing new to relate   The departments active

04.07.1864   Received orders to cook and keep on hand four days' rations and be ready to start at any time

04.08.1864   All very quiet   Quite cold for the season

04.09.1864   A portion of the command moving and changing positions

(There is no entry for April 10, 1864)

04.11.1864   Started our march   Traveled west   Passed through Brownsville, Haywood County, TN and encamped with orders to be ready to start at two AM A rainy night.

04.12.1864   We arrived at Fort Pillow and attacked the same early in the day   The fort was defended by about 450 blacks and 250 whites   We captured about 40 blacks & 100 whites and killed the remainder   We demolished the place

04.13.1864[52]   After taking possession of the commissaries and ordinance stores and removing the same, we started back toward Jackson and encamped for the night near Brownsville.

04.14.1864[53]   Continued our march and arrived at Jackson having traveled about 140 miles in four days, fought eight hours, killed 500 yanks and negroes, and captured six pieces of artillery with all of their stores

04.15.1864   Remained at Jackson waiting for the command to come up with all of their goods and stores   General Buford went into Paducah, capturing a large lot of horses

04.16.1864   Remained at Jackson   Received orders to prepare rations and be ready to start the next morning

04.17.1864   The order countermanded and we remained at Jackson   Balls quite fashionable the last week   I went to the Episcopalian Church

04.18.1864   The command remained at Jackson   Twenty of the company went south as an escort to Governor I.G. Harris

04.19.1864   Talking of going south daily but we are here with a better prospect of staying   Details of the company going south daily

04.20.1864   Remained at Jackson   The command very busily getting up conscripts, deserters, horse thieves, etc.

---

52   *See Appendix IV*
53   *See Appendix IV*

04.21.1864   Remained at Jackson   Daily arrival of conscripts and deserters   A great many volunteering   The command increasing rapidly

04.22.1864   Remained at Jackson Nothing new The command continues in the same business

04.23.1864   All quiet without any change   A heavy rain in the PM

04.24.1864   Remained at Jackson   All quiet   I went to church Considerable activity in the conscript department

04.25.1864   Remained at Jackson   The weather assumes the appearance of spring -warm and beautiful

04.26.1864   Remained at Jackson   Nothing new

04.27.1864   Remained at Jackson   All quiet, with the exception of the conscripts, which is very active   Evening rides with ladies quite fashionable

04.28.1864   Remained at Jackson   Arrival of conscripts daily Some preparation for a march   Balls given nearly every night

04.29.1864   Remained at Jackson   Received orders to prepare five days' rations and be ready to leave on the first of May   Heavy rains

04.30.1864   Remained at Jackson   Attended a picnic given by Miss Mollie Hubbard's School - moved to the Maness' house in consequence of a rain and went to dancing.

May 1864

05.01.1864   The order was postponed and we remained on account of heavy rains the day before   The wagons and a portion of the command started Attended the burial of [54]Colonel Wiley Reed Went to Church

05.02.1864   Started our march   Crossed the Hatchie River at Bolivar, TN Had a light engagement with the enemy at Bolivar and then moved off leaving two killed

05.03.1864   Continued our march south Went near Bolivar and encamped

05.04.1864   Pursued our course toward Tupelo, MS arriving within eight miles of there and encamped for the night

05.05.1864   We arrived at Tupelo, having traveled between 40 and 50 miles per day carrying two days' forage for our horses and four days' ration for men

05.06.1864   Remained near Tupelo resting and recruiting our stock which are in bad condition On duty today

05.07.1864   Remained at Tupelo Nothing to relate Spent the time entertaining my distinguished guest *(?)*

05.08.1864   Remained at Tupelo News from the Trans Mississippi Department and the Army of Northern Virginia very good

05.09.1864   Remained at Tupelo The news from the rebel army continues favorable

---

54   *(Bradley, 2006), pp. 108-109.*

05.10.1864   Remained at Tupelo   All the news favorable to the rebels

05.11.1864   Remained at Tupelo   All quiet   The weather warm in the day, but very cold at night

05.12.1864   Remained at Tupelo   The news from Virginia, Dalton, GA, and the Trans Mississippi very favorable Wrote a letter to my wife

05.13.1864   No change in camp   Remained at the same place Going through the regular routine of duty

05.14.1864   Remained at Tupelo   A general review today   All passed off well

05.15.1864   Remained at Tupelo   All quiet in camp   Great eagerness to get the news

05.16.1864   Remained at Tupelo Great eagerness to get the news, which is quite favorable from the Trans Mississippi Department and the Virginia Army Received orders to prepare five days' rations and be ready to march

05.17.1864   The order countermanded and we remained at Tupelo

05.18.1864   Remained at Tupelo The news from every department of the army continues to be very cheering

05.19.1864   Remained at Tupelo   Going through the regular routine of duty   The news continues good

05.20.1864   No change in the command   The news continues favorable

05.21.1864   Remained at Tupelo   No change in the command
               The weather warm and dry

05.22.1864   Remained at Tupelo   Considerable activity with the
               command preparing for a march

05.23.1864   Received orders to prepare for a march the next
               day   The order countermanded and we remained at
               Tupelo

05.24.1864   Remained at Tupelo   Received orders for thirty of
               the company to be ready to start the next morning

05.25.1864   Thirty of the company went toward Ripley, MS on
               a scout hunting some deserters   The remainder of
               the company remained at Tupelo

05.26.1864   Remained at Tupelo   Going through the regular
               routine of duty

05.27.1864   Remained at Tupelo   The thirty that had gone off
               scouted the woods over in the neighborhood of
               Ripley capturing fifteen deserters and returned

05.28.1864   Remained at Tupelo   Nothing of interest occurred

05.29.1864   Remained at Tupelo   Received orders to prepare
               rations and be ready to move in the morning, but
               before night the order was countermanded

05.30.1864   Remained at Tupelo   Everything very active
               Preparing for a march News from Virginia and
               Georgia very exciting

05.31.1864   Remained at Tupelo Orders to be ready to start the next morning The command very active preparing for a move

෨

June 1864

06.01.1864   Started on our march Traveled northeast through Fulton, Ms and encamped

06.02.1864   Continued our march Crossed the Mississippi and Alabama state line and encamped, our average travel being about thirty five miles per day

06.03.1864   Started on our march Went to Frankfort, AL Received orders changing the program Our orders being countermanded, we turned right about and took up our march back on the same road

06.04.1864   Pursued our course back on the same road Traveled very hard and encamped near Mooreville, MS It has been raining ever since we left Tupelo

06.05.1864   Started early and went to Tupelo for breakfast Arrived here greatly fatigued and very muddy. Received orders to get everything in order to start the next morning at daylight

06.06.1864   Remained at Tupelo resting and preparing for a march Our order for a march suspended until the next day

06.07.1864   Started on our march Went north along the railroad and encamped at Baldwyn, MS Very heavy rains and the waters high

06.08.1864   Continued our march along the railroad and encamped at Booneville, MS It continues to rain daily

06.09.1864   Went on a reconnaissance with General S.D. Lee and General Forrest around about Reinzi, MS and returned to Booneville The Yanks are advancing and General Forrest is maneuvering his troops Two men from Kentucky shot for desertion

06.10.1864   About 10 AM the fight began near [55]Brice's Cross Roads, five miles from Guntown, MS, which lasted until four in the afternoon, when we routed them We pressed them heavily, following them until 10 PM

06.11.1864   After resting about three hours during the night we started at one AM, overtaking their rear at Big Hatchie River Fighting commenced and we skirmished with them from there to [56]Salem, MS They were completely demoralized & threw away their guns and accouterments They traveled 60 miles in 24 hours

----

55   *Brice's Cross Roads is now Bethany, Mississippi (Mississippi Atlas & Gazetteer, 2007)*
56   *There are now four communities in Mississippi known as Salem. The Salem Dyer refers to here is now New Salem, Mississippi in Itawamba County (Mississippi Atlas & Gazetteer, 2007)*

06.12.1864   We deployed through the woods and skirmished through the woods back to Ripley, having in the past two days killed about 500, wounded 600 or 700, captured 1,500 prisoners and scattered the remainder in the woods completely annihilating their 16th Army Corps with only 3,000 men

06.13.1864   We returned to Guntown   1,200 prisoners arrived here today   The command very busily engaged catching stragglers, burying the dead, and removing captured property to this place

06.14.1864   Remained at Guntown removing property from the battlefield to Guntown, which will require several days   Prisoners arriving and being sent to the rear

06.15.1864   Went to Tupelo to rest   It will take one week to remove the captured property, bury the dead, and dispose of the prisoners   Our wounded sent to [57]Lauderdale Spring, MS

06.16.1864   Remained at Tupelo   General Forrest went to Columbus, MS Prisoners passing down the road

[58](*a page of the diary is missing*)

06.23.1864   Tupelo, MS   Nothing of importance has transpired for several days   Flags of truce going to Memphis, TN to consult about the negro troops, their treatment, etc.

---

57   *Lauderdale Spring was a health resort and spa near present day Lauderdale, MS . During the Civil War it was converted to a Confederate hospital (Geocities.com, 2008)*

58   *See Appendix IV*

06.24.1864   Remained at Tupelo   The weather very warm and dry   Everything very dull

06.25.1864   Remained at Tupelo   No change to relate   The second flag of truce started to Memphis   Wrote a letter home to my wife

06.26.1864   All very quiet   The weather warm and sultry   One flag of truce returned

06.27.1864   Remained at Tupelo   Nothing new to relate   It continues very warm and sultry

06.28.1864   Remained at Tupelo   Very warm and sultry   The news from GA very encouraging   All very quiet here   Flag of truce returned

06.29.1864   Remained at Tupelo   Warm and sultry   Some indications of a move   The different departments very active   Another flag of truce left here this morning, which makes the 4th since the 10th of this month

06.30.1864   All very quiet today   Scouts report the Federals at LaGrange, TN in heavy force   They are repairing the road from Memphis, TN toward Corinth, MS

                                            ᐧᑌᕮ

July 1864

07.01.1864   Remained at Tupelo, MS   All very quiet   Warm and sultry

07.02.1864   Remained at Tupelo   No change to relate   The Federals are at LaGrange, TN   Both parties watching each other's movements

07.03.1864   No change to relate   All quiet   Went to church   Very warm

07.04.1864   Remained at Tupelo   Nothing new to relate   All quiet

07.05.1864   All quiet   Remained at the same place   Going through the regular routine of duty

07.06.1864   Remained at Tupelo   Received orders to prepare rations and be ready to march the next morning

07.07.1864   The order suspended and we remained at Tupelo

07.08.1864   Started on our march   Went to Okolona, MS and encamped   Very warm

(There are no entries for [59] July 9th and 10th)

07.11.1864   Remained at Okolona   Everything very active Preparing for active operations   Warm and sultry - a heavy rain

07.12.1864   Remained at Okolona until 4 PM, then started on the Pontotoc Road   Traveled until 11 PM and encamped within seven miles of Pontotoc, MS

---

59   *See Appendix IV*

07.13.1864   The Federals moved out from Pontotoc on the Tupelo Road   We commenced skirmishing with them at Pontotoc and followed them on the Tupelo Road, fighting them through the day   BT Arnold was wounded and died

07.14.1864   Heavy firing during the day near [60]Harrisburg, MS We were repulsed Also fighting on the Verona Road after dark   We were repulsed   Loss on both sides very heavy   The Yanks held the battlefield   The weather very warm and many *(left blank)* fainting

07.15.1864   Heavy skirmishing commenced early in the morning The Federals moved off early in the morning on the Ellistown Road   We were pressing very close [61]General Forrest was wounded in the foot

07.16.1864   Moved out with the expectation of having another fight, but the Yanks moved off in the direction of Ripley, MS and we returned   Generals Chalmers & Roddey pursuing them

07.17.1864   Moved from Tupelo to Okolona   The weather extremely warm

07.18.1864   Remained at Okolona resting   All quiet

07.19.1864   Remained at Okolona   Nothing to relate   All quiet

---

60   *In 1864 Harrisburg and Tupelo were apparently two distinct communities very close together, which have now become one, known as Tupelo, Mississippi (Mississippi Atlas & Gazetteer, 2007)*

61   *"He was shot in the right foot near the base of the great toe. This proved to be the most painful wound of all. The ball ranged backward through his sole producing a flesh wound. When the severe hemorrhage was finally stopped, he mounted his horse and rode in front of his men." (Welsh, 1995) p. 71*

07.20.1864   Moved our camp to a new place   Water very scarce
              at Okolona

07.21.1864   Remained at Okolona in our new camps   All quiet
              Very dry

07.22.1864   Remained at Okolona   All quiet

07.23.1864   Remained at Okolona   All quiet   General Forrest
              started for Columbus, MS

07.24.1864   I started for Columbus, MS   Passed through
              Meridian, MS and encamped

07.25.1864   Continued our march and arrived at Columbus at
              noon   Put up our horses at Lady's Stable and we
              remained in town

07.26.1864   Remained in Columbus luxuriating in fruits, melons,
              etc.   All quiet

07.27.1864   Remained in Columbus   Passing off the time very
              pleasantly

07.28.1864   I rode into the country   Passing off the time very
              pleasantly

07.29.1864   I returned to Columbus to join the squad that was
              there with the General   Very warm and sultry   An
              occasional shower of rain

07.30.1864   Remained at Columbus with the General   Received
              orders to be ready to start back to the command the
              next morning

07.31.1864   Started to the command at Okolona   Went to
             Meridian and encamped

∽

August 1864

08.01.1864   Continued our march and arrived at Okolona   Very
             heavy rain

08.02.1864   Remained at Okolona   Received orders to prepare
             for a march

08.03.1864   The order suspended and we remained at Okolona
             A portion of the command went to the front

08.04.1864   Remained at Okolona   All quiet   The command
             luxuriating in watermelons, etc.

08.05.1864   Remained at Okolona going through the regular
             routine of duty

08.06.1864   Remained at the same place   Preparing for a
             march

08.07.1864   Remained at Okolona   Received orders to prepare
             for a march and be ready to start the next morning
             (left blank) o'clock

08.08.1864   Started on our march   The order countermanded
             and we returned to the same place with orders to be
             ready to start the next morning at 4 AM

08.09.1864   Started on our march   Went to Pontotoc   Moved from Pontotoc northwest   Traveled twelve miles and encamped at [62]Buttermilk Springs

08.10.1864   Pursued our journey passing by Lafayette Springs, MS, arriving at Oxford late at night, the enemy having evacuated the same in the evening

08.11.1864   Remained at Oxford   Collecting and dispersing of troops

(The diary ends here)

⚜

---

62   *(Mississippi Atlas & Gazetteer, 2007)*

Forrest's Farewell Address To His Command

Gainesville, Ala May 9, 1865

CIVIL WAR, SUCH AS YOU HAVE PASSED THROUGH, NATURALLY ENGENDERS FEELINGS OF ANIMOSITY, HATRED AND REVENGE. IT IS OUR DUTY TO DIVEST OURSELVES OF ALL SUCH FEELINGS, AND, SO FAR AS IT IS IN OUR POWER TO DO SO, TO CULTIVATE FRIENDLY FEELINGS TOWARD THOSE WITH WHOM WE HAVE SO LONG CONTESTED AND HERETOFORE SO WIDELY BUT HONESTLY DIFFERED. NEIGHBORHOOD FEUDS, PERSONAL ANIMOSITIES, AND PRIVATE DIFFERENCES SHOULD BE BLOTTED OUT, AND WHEN YOU RETURN HOME A MANLY STRAIGHTFORWARD COURSE OF CONDUCT WILL SECURE YOU THE RESPECT EVEN OF YOUR ENEMIES.

I HAVE NEVER ON THE FIELD OF BATTLE SENT YOU WHERE I WAS UNWILLING TO GO MYSELF, NOR WOULD I NOW ADVISE YOU TO A COURSE WHICH I MYSELF FELT UNWILLING TO PURSUE. YOU HAVE BEEN GOOD SOLDIERS. YOU CAN BE GOOD CITIZENS.

N.B. FORREST, LIEUTENANT GENERAL

APPENDIX I – PERSONS MENTIONED

NAME	DIARY DATE(S)
Armstrong, Frank Crawford	05.29.1863, 09.14.1863
Arnold, B.T.	07.13.1864
Balding, Jim	01.23.1863
Boone, Nathaniel	07.11.1863, 08.06.1863
Bragg, Braxton	06.24.1863, 07.03.1863, 09.13.1863, 09.14.1863, 09.18.1863, 09.20.1863, 09.21.1863, 09.22.1863, 09.23.1863, 10.03.1863, 10.08.1863, 10.09.1863, 10.20.1863, 10.29.1863, 10.30.1863
Buford, Abraham	04.15.1864
Bullock, Len	01.02.1863
Chalmers, James Ronald	07.16.1864
Cheatham, Benjamin Franklin	10.28.1863
Davis, Jefferson	08.21.1863, 10.09.1863
Dean, T.P.	06.30.1863
Dibrell, George Gibbs	04.19.1863, 10.20.1863
Edmonson, James Howard	04.19.1863
Faulkner, W.W.	03.23.1864
Forrest, Jeffrey E.	02.22.1864
Forrest, Nathan Bedford	05.13.1863, 06.13.1863, 06.24.1863, 07.11.1863, 07.23.1863, 07.24.1863, 07.31.1863, 08.01.1863, 08.06.1863, 08.25.1863, 08.26.1863, 09.11.1863, 09.22.1863, 09.25.1863, 09.28.1863, 10.01.1863, 10.10.1863, 10.13.1863, 10.16.1863, 10.17.1863, 10.20.1863, 10.21.1863, 10.22.1863, 10.29.1863, 10.30.1863, 10.31.1863, 11.01.1863, 12.06.1863, 12.16.1863, 12.26.1863, 01.04.1864, 01.17.1864, 01.18.1864, 01.19.1864, 01.29.1864, 01.31.1864, 02.12.1864, 02.23.1864, 02.28.1864, 06.09.1864, 06.16.1864, 07.15.1864, 07.23.1864, 07.29.1864, 07.30.1864
Gould, Andrew Wills	06.13.1863
Harris, Isham Green	04.18.1864

NAME	DIARY DATE(S)
Holt, Joshua	02.21.1864
Hubbard, Mollie	04.30.1864
Hurlburt, Stephen Augustus	01.18.1864, 01.19.1864
Jones, Theodore	01.14.1863
Lee, Robert Edward	07.10.1863
Lee, Stephen Dill	12.01.1863, 06.09.1894
Livingston, W.H.	02.22.1864
Longstreet, James	10.28.1863
Lytle, Ad	01.17.1863
Madux, Dan	01.06.1863
Maxwell, R.H.	02.22.1864
Murphy, Jim	01.18.1863
Murse, Arthur	01.13.1863
Pegram, John	09.10.1863, 09.12.1863
Pillow, Gideon Johnson	06.21.1863
Polk, Leonidas	01.04.1864, 01.29.1864, 02.28.1864
Reed, Wiley	05.01.1864
Rhodes, Jazeb R.	09.04.1863
Roddey, Phillip Dale	07.16.1864
Rosecrans, William Starke	08.23.1863, 09.13.1863, 09.14.1863, 09.18.1863, 09.21.1863, 09.22.1863, 09.23.1863
Starnes, James W.	04.05.1863, 06.29.1863, 06.30.1863
Stevenson, Carter Littlepage Jr.	10.19.1863
Streight, Abel D.	05.03.1863
Van Dorn, Earl	03.04.1863
Walker, Mose	01.24.1863
Warren, James M.	02.21.1864
Wheeler, Joseph	09.28.1863, 09.29.1863, 10.12.1863, 10.14.1863
Woodford, Stewart Lyndon	09.26.1863, 09.27.1863

APPENDIX II – LOCATIONS MENTIONED

TENNESSEE	TENNESSEE	ALABAMA	GEORGIA	MISSISSIPPI
Athens	Macon	Ashville	Atlanta	Aberdeen
Bethesda	McDonald	Athens	Cave Spring	Baldwyn
Big Springs	Medon	Bellefonte	Dalton	Bellefontaine
Bolivar	Memphis	Bessemer	Graysville	Booneville
Branchville	Montezuma	Birmingham	Greensport	Buttermilk
Brentwood	Mount Pleasant	Blountsville	Resaca	Springs
Brownsville	Mouse Creek	Bridgeport	Ringgold	Camargo
Charleston	Station	Buckhorn Tavern	Rome	Caledonia
Chattanooga	Nashville	Danville	Tunnel Hill	Coffeeville
Cleveland	Niota	Decatur		Columbus
Collierville	Pelham	Demopolis	**ILLINOIS**	Como
Columbia	Philadelphia	Elyton	Highland Park	Corinth
Cowan	Pinhook	Florence		Ellistown
Decherd	Pocahontas	Frankfort	**KENTUCKY**	Fulton
Dresden	Purdy	Jacksonville	Danville	Grenada
Dukedom	Riggs Crossroads	Jonesboro (Old)	Lexington	Guntown
Eagleville	Roddy	Montgomery	Mayfield	Harrisburg
Estanaula	Rossville	Mooresville	Paducah	Hendersonville
Elkton	Salem (Old	Moulton		Holly Springs
Fayette Station	Salem)	New Market	**SOUTH**	Hudsonville
Franklin	Saulsbury	Pikeville	**CAROLINA**	Jackson
Georgetown	Shelbyville	Scottsboro	Charleston	Lauderdale
Harrison	Somerville	Springville		Spring
Hillville	Spring Creek	Stevenson	**VIRGINIA**	Lafayette Springs
Humboldt	Spring Hill	Tredegar	Portsmouth	Meridian
Jackson	Sweetwater	Turkeytown		Mooreville
Kingston	Thompson's	Tuscaloosa		New Albany
Knoxville	Station	Woodville		New Salem
LaGrange	Trenton			Okolona
Loudon	Triune			Oxford
	Tullahoma			Pontotoc
	Union City			Reinzi
	Unionville		**WISCONSIN**	Ripley
	Winchester		Racine	Salem
	Windrow			Starkville
	Wood			Thaxton
				Tupelo
				Verona
				Vicksburg
				Water Valley
				West Point
				Wyatt

APPENDIX III – THE FORREST/ GOULD AFFAIR

Article appearing in the Nashville Banner April 29, 1911:

[63]THE PERSONAL ENCOUNTER–
GENERAL FORREST AND LIEUT. GOULD

War Tragedy in Columbia, Tennessee June 13, 1863—Details given by Man Who as a Boy Witnessed the Conflict— Forrest's Towering Rage when he thought He was Mortally Wounded—Gould Thought His Transfer to another Command a Reflection on His Courage— Grew out of Streight Raid in North Alabama

---

By Frank H. Smith, Secretary of Maury County Historical Society

The old Masonic Hall set back of Seventh and Garden streets some eight or ten feet, making a small yard, then enclosed by a stone and iron fence. Three broad stone steps led from an inside pavement to the large front door, which was at that time open; there was a central hall, closed at the north end; on the east and west of the hall were

---

63　(Nashville Banner, 1911)

four rooms used by Forrest as headquarters or as offices by some of his staff.

On the afternoon of June 13, 1863, four boys were passing this building, the writer being one of them. We saw Gen. Forrest in the hall, and with boyish curiosity we went up the steps and standing on the broad step almost in the door we saw the whole affair.

Forrest and Gould were in the hall talking in rather low tones, but excited. Gould had on a long linen coat something like the modern khaki uniform; he was standing near the door of the east room (which was closed), while Forrest was nearer the front door. About the time we boys got to the top step Gould said something like "It's false." Or "That's all false." Gould told his kinsman, Sam Lee of Duplex, Tennessee that he had said to Forrest that the charges were false, and that the General must have understood him as reflecting on him personally.

Forrest had (or put) his left hand in his trousers' pocket, threw forward his left hand, and crouching his head low looked intently at Gould. Without glancing at the penknife he had in the left hand, he opened it with his teeth and started towards the Lieutenant. Meanwhile Gould was attempting to draw his pistol from his coat pocket. Forrest caught him by the right wrist, which turned the pistol up, and plunged the blade of the knife into Gould's right side between the ribs. All this happened nearly at the same instance and in less time than it takes to write it. Gould wrenched himself loose and made a break for the door and ran up the street towards the

Square. By this time some of the officers came into the hall and caught the General as he reached the steps.

The Surgeon's Story

Dr. James H. Wilkes, who now lives here and Dr. Luke Ridley of Murfreesboro were surgeons in charge of the hospital at the Corinthian Hall (now the Andrews' Public School), and having finished their afternoon rounds, were coming up town. When at the Phoenix Bank corner they saw the excitement down the street and heard Maj. C. S. Severson (Forrest's Quartermaster) crying out: "Stop that man! Stop that man! He's shot Gen. Forrest": they saw a wounded man crossing the street and could see the blood spurting against his linen coat. Dr. Ridley said: "My God, it's Wills Gould," and hastening their steps, they caught him just as he reached the pavement at the Provost Marshall's office, now Turner's grocery.

Supporting him on each side, they walked up the pavement to the first open door, which was Oakes and Engle's Tailor Shop, and helped him up the steps. This was a very short building, and like many of the other old stores the floor was about two feet higher than now, the entrance being by stone steps on this pavement. There were merchandise counters on the east and west sides, while across the rear end (South) was a wide, low table, on which the tailors sat. The corners of this low table connected with the corners of the counters; at the southwest corner of the store was a back door with a very high step into a narrow alley.

Dressing Gould's Wound

Dr. Wilkes and Dr. Ridley led Gould to the back door and laid him on the floor. Dr. Ridley said he would go for surgical appliances and compresses, and in answer to many questions said that Gould would probably die. We boys had pushed our way until we came plumb against the low table. By this time Dr. Wilkes had decided to put Gould on the table where he could better dress the wound; he assisted Gould to his feet, and almost unaided the latter turned and sat down on the low table. Dr. Wilkes took off Gould's linen coat, the right pocket showing the powder-burn of the shot fired at Forrest, and laid Gould on the table, his face turned slightly towards the front door. When the shirt was rolled up under the armpit the stab between the ribs was plainly visible; as he breathed the blood would spurt out, often spattering us boys, but we could hardly dodge, there was such a crown behind us. The intercostal artery was cut, and Dr. Wilkes was bending over him trying to staunch it with his fingers while waiting for Dr. Ridley to bring the proper surgical appliances.

Provost Marshall's Recollections

Col J. Lee Bullock was the Provost Marshall, his office being where Turner's Grocery is now, and which building had not then been lengthened; in the rear was a little frame or log cabin occupied by an old negro named "Gume" Kennedy. Col. Bullock writes me from Washington that he had previously heard that Forrest had accused Gould of cowardice, and that the Lieutenant had demanded an investigation which the General was not inclined to grant. When Col. Bullock saw the excitement on the street he ran out, meeting Gould, running and weakening from loss of blood. Later seeing Forrest across the street he met the General just as the latter got off the pavement there, and tried to dissuade Forrest, saying: "I think you need not pursue Gould for I believe that he is fatally wounded; he is bleeding profusely and losing strength with every step." Forrest replied angrily: "Get out of my way, I am mortally wounded and will kill the man who shot me." Mr. A. Nick Akin, now Clerk & Mastery of our Chancery Court, says that just then Forrest seized two pistols from an officer and crossed the street. Col Bullock says that Forrest went down the alley to "Gume" Kennedy's house, but learning that Gould was in the tailor stop, he came back through the alley and went around to the front door of the shop. The late William J. Andrews told me that he had that day loaned a revolver to Capt. John G. Anderson, and that as Forrest was starting up the street to follow Gould, the General took this pistol; but just before reaching the south pavement heard that Gould was mortally wounded and, with some of his officers, went back across the street to Dr. Sam Frierson's who was post surgeon.

The Innocent Bystander

Presently there was a great commotion at the front door of the tailor shop. Forrest came in, very much in dishabille (?), with a revolver in each hand, yelling, "Lookout! Lookout!" Gould evidently saw or heard him and raised up to roll off the low table, the blood spurting over us boys in the effort. Dr. Wilkes also saw Forrest and jumped in the corner out of range. As Gould stepped down out of the back door, Forrest fired, but the ball glanced from the brick wall, striking a "Dutchman" in the leg; he belonged to Gen. Armstrong's escort, and happened to be in the alley; Mr. Jim Fleming of the Zion neighborhood was in town that day, and, not feeling very well, had gone into the shop to take an after-dinner nap. The confusion incident to Gould's being brought into the shop, and the great crowd did not arouse him, and he slept on in blissful ignorance of all this disturbance. But when Forrest fired Mr. Fleming jumped up, shouting, "Somebody's shot the top of my head off"—a remark that did not tend to quiet the excitement.

Forrest Pursues Gould

Gould ran out into the back yard, where there was vigorous growth of high weeds, and fell in them. Forrest, in a torrent of rage, went around the west counter and stepped down into the alley. He followed a little path in the rear of those stores that faced the square. Mr. A.O.B. Nicholson, now United States Marshal of this district, had been ordered by Gen. Bragg to report to Forrest here as drill master, and was then in the back lot. He says that when Forrest saw Gould laying in the weeds the General touched Gould with his foot as if to turn him over, and then returned to the back door of the shop. Forrest straddled over the short corner where the table joined the counter, and went toward the front door, the crowd quickly giving him passageway.

The Carriage Ride

Recognizing Dr. Wilkes at the door the General asked him to go with him, but the doctor told him his first duty was to the wounded man he was attending, but Forrest, with an oath ordered him to go with him. On reaching the pavement Dr. Ridley was met coming with the compresses and surgical appliances, where the same questions were asked and the same answers given as at the door, accompanied by an additional oath from Forrest to get in that carriage. Forrest himself got in unaided, and with Dr. Wilkes and Dr. Ridley the trio went diagonally across the street to Dr. Sam Frierson's and he was added to the party. The quartette was then driven to Maj. William Galloway's on Ninth Street, we boys holding onto the carriage behind. The doctors wanted to assist the General in getting to his room upstairs, but he did not accept their aid; while his language was more guarded his rage was terrible.

Forrest's Wound

As soon as the General was undressed, Dr. Frierson told Dr. Wilkes to probe the wound. [64]Much to their gratification they found that the ball striking the crest of the ileum had gone outside of the bone and was buried in the large glutil muscles of the left hip. The doctors told Forrest that it was a mere flesh wound and that the ball could be cut out. "no," said Forrest, "it's nothing but a d___ little pistol ball, let it alone"—and they let it alone. (I am informed that Dr. Cowan later cut it out at Huntsville).

Dr. Wilkes tells me that as soon as Forrest learned the nature of the wound his whole demeanor changed and his rage vanished. Without waiting for the wound

---

64 *A modern-day description of Forrest's wound at the hands of Lieutenant Gould is found in (Welsh, 1995) p. 71:*

"...Gould shot Forrest at close range with a large caliber pistol... The bullet entered just above his left hip joint and struck the outer edge of the pelvic bone below the anterior superior spinous process. It was deflected upward and passed back through his body without having touched his intestines or any large blood vessels."

to be dressed he told Dr. Ridley to go at once to his kinsman, and if Gould was not dead, have him taken to the Nelson House and tell Joe walker to give him the best room in the hotel and every attention and that he would be responsible for all expenses; he also told Dr. Ridley to give his case his personal care and do all he could for him. He ended by saying: "And by God, Ridley, when I give such an order I mean it" Dr. Ridley at once returned to town in the carriage, but Gould had already been carried to the Nelson House under guard, I think, by Capt. Henry Smith of Forrest's staff. After Dr. Ridley left Dr. Frierson and Dr. Wilkes dressed the wound. Up to this time they knew nothing of the circumstances, and Forrest of his own accord told his account of this difficulty.

Forrest's Version

He said that he was at headquarters that afternoon picking his teeth with a small penknife, when Gould was announced. Not dreaming of any personal difficulty he closed the knife and stepped into the hall where the conversation would be more private. Gould said: "Gen. Forrest , did you give this order ?" Forrest took the paper, read it and said, "Yes I did." Gould replied that he wanted an explanation of such an order, and Forrest interrupted him by saying that his mind was made up and he did not care to discuss the matter. Gould said that it might be construed as an imputation of cowardice, and "no man can accuse me of cowardice and both of us live." Forrest said that Gould made a motion to draw a pistol from his pocket, but it hung there, and Gould fired before it was out of his pocket; that he grabbed Gould's hand to prevent another shot, opened the knife with his teeth, and stabbed Gould as the latter slipped by Forrest also said that he had borrowed a pistol after getting out of the Masonic Building and started up the street, when understanding that Dr. Ridley reported that the lieutenant was mortally wounded he had gone to Sam Frierson's office to have his own wound dressed. Dr. Frierson had barely seen the wound, and being asked as to it's nature had said it could not be ascertained except by probing; being persistently questioned he said that from it's location, if the ball had gone inside (as it appeared to have done), and perforated the intestines, it would be apt to prove fatal in that warm weather. Just at that moment Maj. Severson had come in and said, "General, that — scoundrel is not much hurt. I saw him walking around in the back of the tailor's shop."

Forrest said that he grabbed two pistols from an officer and without waiting to rearrange all of his clothing he rushed out saying he would kill him before he died. In further talking Forrest said that if Gould had shown as much bravery on the battlefield as he had shown that afternoon this affair would have not happened.

Forrest showed the knife. It was quite small, with a long, narrow blade, very keen. It had been captured at Franklin on June 4th, in the suttler's supplies. Dr Wilkes washed the blood from it and returned it to the General.

Dr. Frierson and Dr. Wilkes visited Forrest every day until he left a few days later. He always made inquiries about Gould.

Nursing Forrest

Mrs. Minnie Galloway Towler tells me of an incident that happened the next day after the shooting. Her mother had prepared a broth for the General, and with her childish desire to do something she had carried it to him herself. As she approached the bed she stumbled and spilled the bowl of hot broth on him; he jumped with an exclamation, but seeing her tears he quickly subsided and apologized. Forrest and other Confederate officers were always welcome guests at Maj. Galloway's home, where more than one council of war was held by the Generals. The east room upstairs was known as Gen. Forrest's.

Nursing Gould

The Lieutenant was carried to the second story of the Nelson House (then the leading hotel of Maury County) and given the best room; it was on the west front opening on a narrow verandah. Mr. Sam Lee writes that he obtained permission to wait on his kinsman, and that he remained with Gould from 4 o'clock in the afternoon of his difficulty until his death. The wound had been dressed when Lee arrived. A guard was placed at the door with orders to admit no one except the surgeon and the nurses. When Lee was unavoidably absent, the guard sometimes waited on Gould. Three days before Gould's death his half-brother, Foster Gould, came to Columbia and called in another surgeon, Dr. J.M. Towler, who said that he had healed from the outside and that death was inevitable. Gould told Mr. Lee that as Forrest stabbed him he then fired; that he did not shoot again, as he had no desire to kill Forrest, but merely to protect himself.

As To Reconciliation

It has long been the impression in Columbia that Forrest and Gould became reconciled, though Mr. Sam Lee says that he cannot recall that Forrest ever came to Gould's room. Many years ago in reading this sketch to the only other eye-witness then living, Mr. Eugene Pillow, he recalled an interview between his father and General Forrest a few days after the difficulty. Dr. Pillow had called on Forrest socially, and the General said that he had been misinformed as to the facts and mistaken in his estimate of Gould; that he intended going to see him and tell him so. Dr. Wilkes tells me that Forrest made the same statement to him and Dr. Frierson.

Gould's Death

Dr. Wilkes says that Gould died from traumatic pneumonia as a result of the wound in the right lung, and not as stated in some well-known publications "from septic peritonitis which followed a perforation of the intestine;" for the peritoneum had not been perforated. In the Maury County Historical Society is the account book of Lamb & Barr, undertakers, which shows cash received for Lieutenant Gould's coffin $128.00. The remains were removed to Nashville and are buried in the family lot in the old City Cemetery. A plain headstone has been simply lettered as:

A.W. Gould
Born July 12th, 1840
Died June 26th, 1863

Did Authorities Ignore It!

There is no mention of this case in the Official Records of the Rebellion. As the Confederate forces withdrew from Middle Tennessee in less than a month and did not again occupy this section except for about three weeks in Hood's campaign a year and a half later, nothing seems to have been done about it by the Richmond authorities. If any investigation was ever made I can find no account of it.

Sketch of Lieut. Gould

Andrews Wills Gould was born in Nashville and was the only child of James Gould by his second wife, who was a Miss Wills. His family was related to the Napiers and Hoges of Maury County, and to many other prominent families of Tennessee. After attending local schools he took a three years' course at Cumberland University at Lebanon, graduating with honors in 1861; he then entered the Military Academy at Nashville under Gen. Bushrod Johnson, which he left to join the army.

He was a man of fine personal appearances and captivating manners; he was five feet ten or eleven inches tall, weighing about a hundred and sixty pounds, athletic, and of soldierly bearing. His comrades speak in high terms of his gallantry. Gen. George W. Gordon of Memphis wrote that "as a civilian, a citizen, a man, and a friend I never knew or heard aught of his prejudice; he was a courteous and a refined gentleman of temperate and moral habits."

He enlisted in a battalion of cavalry commanded by his cousin, Col. Alonzo Napier, which captured a Federal transport on the Tennessee River, from which two pieces of artillery wire obtained; they were mounted and placed in charge of Gould. Napier's Battalion joined Forrest in his first expedition into West Tennessee in November 1862. When Morton's Battery was organized at Dresden Gould's section was incorporated in it and he became first Lieutenant. The campaign closed by Forrest escaping across the Tennessee River and returning to Mt. Pleasant and later Columbia.

In February 1863, while the command was reorganizing in Maury County Gould became engaged to one of the most beautiful and attractive young ladies who ever attended the Athenaeum; she is still unmarried and keeps his memory in holy reverence.

Freeman's Battery

Another battery of Forrest's was commanded by Capt. Sam Freeman of Nashville. In an engagement on the Lewisburg and Franklin Pike near Douglass Church on April 10, 1863 Freeman had been killed (it is said after he surrendered), and Lieuts. Huggins and Baxter captured with many of the men; but the Federals did not succeed in removing the guns from the field, though they disabled the battery by cutting the spokes. It was thought that Gould would be given this battery after the death of Freeman, but the plum fell to Huggins, who was exchanged about the middle of May. Even this early there was a rivalry among the officers for Forrest's favor, which in some instances became almost a jealousy.

The Streight Raid

In Streight's raid in North Alabama, which added such laurels to Forrest's fame, Gould commanded a section of a battery. In the fight on Sand Mountain, near Day's Gap, on the last day of April 1863 the Federal line was in ambush in a ravine. Forrest had sent off part of his command by a circular route to gain another pass into the mountains, retaining with him only a newly organized Eleventh Tennessee Cavalry, Gould's two guns, and Capt. Bill Forrest's Fourth Scouts.

Probably no general in all history used artillery as daringly as Forrest did, often advancing a battery on a skirmish line, and in this affair the Confederates' advance was accompanied by Gould's two twelve-pounder brass howitzers.

Forrest seems to have gone right into the trap, and when the Federals rose from ambush and delivered such a withering fire the Confederates retreated. Mr. Joe Bellanfant of Culleoka says that Gould remained at his guns until every man had left and his own fine black mare was killed. All the horses being killed or so tangled up in the harness that the guns could not be withdrawn, Gould then retreated leaving the guns in the hands of the enemy. Forrest was not only enraged at the loss of the only two cannons with him, but was concerned about the wounding of his brother, Capt. Bill Forrest, whose thigh had been broken by a minnie ball right at Gould's gun. It must not be forgotten that Forrest's only military training was in the school of experience, and until then he had never had such an experience of the tactical advantages of the ambuscade which Streight used so successfully. Charles XII bemoaned the result of his successive victorious campaigns teaching the Russians the art of war; Forrest's common sense did not require a single campaign or a single day to learn to profit by such a lesson, for although Streight used the ambuscade several times on that raid, Forrest avoided every similar attempt to entrap him.

It has been said that the case was reported to Forrest in a manner that did not do Gould justice, and in the stirring events following the capture of Streight and the death of General Van Dorn nothing was done about it.

The Fight At Franklin

On June 4th Forrest moved north from Spring Hill with Armstrong's and Starnes' Brigades and two batteries to attack Franklin, then under command of Col. James P. Baird of the Ninety-fifth Indiana. Some two or three miles south of Franklin the Federal pickets were driven or captured, and Forrest pressed on, the fighting continuing from the streets and houses. Most of the Federals took refuge in Fort Granger, across the river, but there were many who remained in the houses in town. Mr. Hardin P. Figures, a leading attorney of Columbia, was then a small boy living in Franklin. He tells me that Gould had three small pieces of artillery, which were stationed on the Carter's Creek Pike, about a hundred yards west of his mother's house; Forrest's object was for this battery to draw the fire from the fort while he captured the town or made a "bluff" inducing the fort to surrender. Gould's cannon were very small and seemed to Mr. Figures like pop guns compared with the heavy artillery in the fort. One of his little balls hit the fort. One struck the arch over the gothic window of the Episcopal Church; another struck the old Presbyterian Church, and another cut a cedar tree in the Female Institute lot, as Gould continued to fire.

Gould succeeded in drawing the fire of the fort. Mr. Figures says one of the immense shells passed just over the battery and plowed a long furrow across Mr. L.H. Moseley's bluegrass lot in the rear of Gould's position, and the battery was moved to the west, where it was better protected. It is said that Forrest was provoked at this, but he continued on in the town, capturing military and sutlers' supplies; he also battered down the doors of the jail, freeing many political prisoners. Armstrong's Brigade, that was east of town, was driven back across the river, and Forrest was soon s.helled out of Franklin.

In the official reports there were no reports from the Confederate side about this engagement, and only three from the Federals.

The Affair At Triune
Just a week later Forrest, with his light artillery attacked the Federals at Triune. It was not his intention to do more than make a reconnaissance in force, but as usual, he did not return empty-handed, and when he returned to Spring Hill and Columbia he had a large drove of beef cattle that had been captured. As in the Franklin fight of the previous Thursday, there are no reports in the Official Records from the Confederates of this affair; the Federal reports show a glorious victory – but don't allude to the beef cattle. Most of the command returned to Spring Hill or Columbia after the Triune fight of the 11th to

recruit and refit. Gould and his artillery mess were stationed on East Hill just across the cedar bridge.

About noon on June 13th, Capt. John W. Morton, Forrest's Chief of artillery, came to the quarters of the mess with an order from Forrest for Gould to report to Gen. Bragg at Tullahoma for assignment to duty. This meant severance from the command which he had been identified with, and it was felt by Gould and the mess as a disgrace. Gould said he would go to headquarters to see about it. He borrowed from one of his messmates (Bill H. Wilkerson of Nashville) a small six-shooter Colt's revolver which was loaded with powder and ball. Mr. Joe Bellanfant of Culleoka, who belonged to this mess, tells me that this was not in good working order, but would sometimes hang in revolving.

Gould left at once for town, and on inquiring at the Masonic Building was told that the General was at dinner at Maj. Galloway's. Going there the door bell was answered by one of the children who was told that an officer wanted to speak with General Forrest. The General left the dinner table and was heard to say: "I'll see you at headquarters at 3 o'clock", and then slammed the door and returned to the table. What happened afterwards has been told already.

APPENDIX IV –
CONTEMPORARY
NEWSPAPER ARTICLES

Note that newspaper accounts lag one to three or more months behind events recorded in Dyer's diary.

JULY 21, 1863– DAILY INTELLIGENCER (ATLANTA, GA)

The undersigned committee appointed to arrange for the reception and entertainment of Gen. Forrest, report that they have procured rooms at the Trout House, at which place his friends and fellow-citizens, ladies of course included, can visit him on tomorrow(Tuesday)from half-past 9 o'clock, to half-past 11 o'clock, A.M.

James M. Calhoun
S.B. Oatman   Committee
J.E. Williams
A.C. Wyly

AUGUST 25, 1863– MEMPHIS COMMERCIAL APPEAL

In an appeal to Southerners, General Forrest has announced that he is sadly in need of 100 artillery horses to replace those in his division completely broken down by the active service of his corps.

OCTOBER 28, 1863– MEMPHIS COMMERCIAL APPEAL

Reports are current throughout the South that Gen. Nathan Bedford Forrest has submitted his resignation to the War Department, after mature deliberation, because of serious disagreements with his ranking superiors. If some step is not promptly taken to end these difficulties at once, the result will be disastrous because the South cannot spare him.

October 30, 1863- Memphis Commercial Appeal

Gen. Nathan Bedford Forrest has arrived in Atlanta where he informed editors of The Appeal that he is somewhat improved in health but does not consider himself able to resume active service in the field. He said his resignation has not been accepted by the War Department in Richmond.

November 14, 1863- Memphis Commercial Appeal

It has been learned that Brig. Gen Nathan Bedford Forrest has been awarded an independent command to act as he sees fit in the Mississippi bottoms. Being a modest man, he is reported to have told President Davis that he does not promise to whip 50,000 Yankees but that he will keep that number busy and very uneasy.

December 19, 1863- Memphis Commercial Appeal

G.W. Adair, aide to General Forrest, is seeking 12 more youths, who will soon be 18 years old and who have good mounts to complete the roster of General Forrest's Escort, one of the best-drilled cavalry units serving the South. He points out that those who have substitutes serving in the army for them by following Forrest now can wipe out the odium of having a "sub".

January 25, 1864- Memphis Commercial Appeal

A private letter to The Appeal at Atlanta reports that General Forrest has defeated two Illinois regiments near Somerville, captured Lafayette, drove the enemy back behind his fortifications at Collierville, captured the wagon train of the 7th Illinois with 60 prisoners, fought the enemy at Jack's Creek, north of Jackson, Tenn., and drove them back.

February 1, 1864- Memphis Commercial Appeal

RICHMOND-President Davis has nominated Nathan Bedford Forrest to be major general of the Confederate forces and the Senate has confirmed the nomination. Forrest is now in Mississippi where he is reported to have made a junction with the forces of General Chalmers at Holly Springs. His recent campaign in West Tennessee is said to have resulted in the addition of 5,000 more men to the Southern forces.

April 10, 1864- Memphis Commercial Appeal
A gentleman who recently left Wyatt, Miss., has reported to The Appeal at Atlanta that General Forrest, after a two-day battle, succeeded in driving more than 200 Yankees into a river and drowning them.

April 13, 1864- Memphis Commercial Appeal
RICHMOND-An official telegram has been received by General Polk from Starkville, Miss. Reporting that General Forrest after severe fighting 10 miles south of Pontotoc succeeded in killing about 50 of the enemy and capturing four or five of his cannon.

June 21, 1864- Memphis Commercial Appeal
Reports have reached The Appeal at Atlanta that General Forrest has captured Union City, Tenn., along with 450 prisoners, among them the renegade Hawkins with most of his regiment.

July 9, 1864- Memphis Commercial Appeal
Mobile citizens are preparing a token of their appreciation to General Forrest in the shape of two Travis guns which are light, easily transported, fired with great rapidity and accuracy, and for the cavalry service, most valuable weapons. One of the guns is already finished.

APPENDIX V – [65]THE GALLOWAY "ESCAPE"

Major Solomon Street had once served under General Chalmers, then been attached to Forrest's command. In the winter of 1862 Street shot and killed William Galloway, a citizen of Saulsbury, Tennessee. Galloway's son, Robert, joined the Confederate army to find Major Street. At Bolivar, Tennessee young Galloway found and killed Major Street and was arrested and placed under guard to await trial.

Those guarding Galloway, being sympathetic to his plight, said loudly in the prisoner's presence that if he attempted to escape "they probably would not be able to hit a running figure in the dark." Of course, Galloway escaped.

Forrest was not amused and had those charged with guarding the prisoner arrested, announcing that he would "shoot every damn one of 'em as soon as the command reached Tupelo." Eventually Captain John Jackson convinced Forrest to reconsider and they were released.

65   (Bradley, 2006) pp. 109–110

APPENDIX VI – ⁶⁶FORREST'S "INTERVIEW" WITH BRAGG

Forrest's chief surgeon, Dr. J.B. Cowan, accompanied the General on a visit to General Braxton Bragg at his headquarters on Missionary Ridge. He left a written record of the details of this remarkable "interview".

"I observed as we rode along that the General was silent, which was unusual with him when we were alone. Knowing him so well, I was convinced that something that displeased him greatly had transpired. He wore an expression which I had seen before on some occasions when a storm was brewing....As we passed the guard in front of the General's tent, I observed that General Forrest did not acknowledge the salute of the sentry, which was so contrary to his custom that I could not but notice it. When we entered the tent where General Bragg was alone, this officer rose from his seat, spoke to Forrest, and, advancing, offered him his hand.

Refusing to take the proffered hand, and standing stiff and erect before Bragg, Forrest said: I am not here to pass civilities or compliments with you, but on other business. You commenced your cowardly and contemptible persecution of me soon after the battle of Shiloh, and you have kept it up ever since. You did it because I reported to Richmond facts, while you reported damned lies. You robbed me of my command in Kentucky, and gave it to one of your

66 (Wyeth, 1959) pp. 242–243

favorites – men that I armed and equipped from the enemies of our country. In a spirit of revenge and spite, because I would not fawn upon you as others did, you drove me into west Tennessee in the winter of 1862, with a second brigade I had organized, with improper arms and without sufficient ammunition, although I had made repeated applications for the same. You did it to ruin me and my career. When in spite of all this I returned with my command, well equipped by captures, you began again your work of spite and persecution, and have kept it up; and now this second brigade, organized and equipped without thanks to you or the government, a brigade which has won a reputation for successful fighting second to none in the army, taking advantage of your position as the commanding general in order to further humiliate me, you have taken these brave men from me.

I have stood your meanness as long as I intend to. You have played the part of a damned scoundrel, and are a coward, and if you were any part of a man I would slap your jaws and force you to resent it. You may as well not issue any more orders to me, for I will not obey them, and I will hold you personally responsible for any further indignities you endeavor to inflict upon me. You have threatened to arrest me for not obeying your orders promptly. I dare you to do it, and say to you that if you ever again try to interfere with me or cross my path it will be at the peril of your life.

The General did not utter a word or move a muscle of his face during this shower of invective from his brigadier..when Forrest had finished he turned his back sharply upon Bragg and stalked out of the tent toward the horses. As they rode away Dr. Cowan remarked, "Well, you are in for it now !" Forrest replied instantly, "He'll never say a word about it; he'll be the last man to mention it; and, mark my word, he'll take no action in the matter. I will ask to be relieved and transferred to a different field, and he will not oppose it."

BIBLIOGRAPHY

BOOKS

Allardice, B. S. *Confederate Colonels, A Biographical Register.* Columbia: University Of Missouri Press. (2008).

Bradley, M. R. *Nathan Bedford Forrest's Escort And Staff.* Gretna: Pelican Publishing Company, Inc. (2006).

Hancock, R.R. *Hancock's Diary or A History of the Second Tennessee Confederate Cavalry.* Nashville: Brandon Printing Company (1887)

Hurst, J. *Nathan Bedford Forrest, A Biography.* New York: Alfred A. Knopf. (1993).

Jordan, General Thomas and Pryor, J.P. *The Campaigns of Lieut.-Gen. N.B. Forrest and of Forrest's Cavalry.* New Orleans and New York: (1868).

Long, E. *The Civil War Day by Day, An Almanac 1861 - 1865.* Garden City: Doubleday & Company, Inc. (1971).

Welsh, J. D. *Medical Histories of Confederate Generals.* Kent: The Kent State University Press. (1995).

Wyeth, John Allan *That Devil Forrest – Life of General Nathan Bedford Forrest.* New York: Harper & Brothers, Publishers (1959).

NEWSPAPERS

Daily Intelligencer (Atlanta, GA) (1863, July 21).

Memphis Commercial Appeal (1863, 1864).

Nashville Banner (1911, April 29).

Richmond Examiner (1863, September 22).

REFERENCE MAPS

Alabama Atlas & Gazetteer. (2006). Yarmouth: DeLorme.

Mississippi Atlas & Gazetteer. (2007). Yarmouth: DeLorme.

Tennessee Atlas & Gazetteer. (2007). Yarmouth: DeLorme.

3405012

Made in the USA